D0474223

From Text Maps to Memory Caps

From Text Maps to Memory Caps

100 *More* Ways to Differentiate Instruction in K–12 Inclusive Classrooms

by

Paula Kluth, Ph.D.

and

Sheila Danaher, M.S.Ed.

·P A U L· H·
BROOKES
PUBLISHING C⚬ ®

Baltimore • London • Sydney

Paul H. Brookes Publishing Co.
Post Office Box 10624
Baltimore, Maryland 21285-0624
USA

www.brookespublishing.com

Copyright © 2014 by Paul H. Brookes Publishing Co., Inc.
All rights reserved.

"Paul H. Brookes Publishing Co." is a registered trademark of
Paul H. Brookes Publishing Co., Inc.

Typeset by Auburn Associates, Inc., Baltimore, Maryland.
Manufactured in the United States of America by
Versa Press, Inc., East Peoria, Illinois.

Corkboard/post-it notes image ©iStockphoto.com/Whiteway.

Illustrations by Barbara Moran. Ms. Moran is a graphic artist, a presenter, a self-advocate, an
advocate for people with disabilities, and a person with autism. Her artwork has been displayed
across the country. Her unique and captivating drawings are available for purchase from
http://www.karlwilliams.com/moran/index.htm

The individuals described in this book are composites or real people whose situations are masked
and are based on the authors' experiences. In all instances, names and identifying details have been
changed to protect confidentiality.

Library of Congress Cataloging-in-Publication Data

Kluth, Paula.
 From text maps to memory caps : 100 more ways to differentiate instruction in k-12 inclusive classrooms / by Paula Kluth, Ph.D.,
and Sheila Danaher, M.S.Ed.
  pages   cm
 ISBN 978-1-59857-360-2
 1. Individualized instruction.   2. Inclusive education.   I. Danaher, Sheila.   II. Title.
 LB1031.K47 2013
 371.9′046—dc23   2013017268

British Library Cataloguing in Publication data are available from the British Library.

2017   2016   2015   2014   2013

10   9   8   7   6   5   4   3   2   1

Contents

Also by Paula Kluth ix
About the Authors. xi
Preface. xiii
Acknowledgments xv

Organization
1   Talk-o-Meters 2
2   Lit Bins 5
3   Month-at-a-Glance Calendar 7
4   Clipboard Corral 9
5   Personalized Learning Agenda 11
6   Protocol Book 13
7   Flexible Grouping Tools 16
8   Helping Hand 18
9   Student-Friendly Storage 20
10   Volunteer Ads. 23

Environment & Sensory
11   Reading Windows 26
12   Visors 28
13   Relaxation Jars 30
14   Weighted Pencils 33
15   Locker Scribbles 36
16   Salt Maps and Figures 38
17   Weighted Snakes. 40
18   Brain Break Bucket. 42
19   Worksheet Peek 45
20   Sensory Book Jackets 47

Technology
21   Book Trailers. 50
22   Word Clouds. 53
23   Community Communicators 55
24   Published Products 58
25   Projected Directions. 60
26   Class and Student Blogs 62
27   5-Minute Stylus. 64
28   Talking Frame 66

29 Tap Light Indicator. 68
30 Tablet Prop 70

Communication & Participation
31 Speech Bubble. 74
32 Handheld Directions 77
33 "Your Turn" Sharing Stick 79
34 Graffiti Table 81
35 Magnetic Poetry 84
36 Dialogue Journals. 86
37 Reading Phones 89
38 Quick Quip Keychains. 91
39 Communication Kits 93
40 Rotating Reader 95

Behavior & Motivation
41 Goal-Setting Cards 98
42 Check-In Tents 100
43 Timers 102
44 Purposeful Puzzles. 105
45 Mantra Reminders 107
46 Classifieds 109
47 Special Interest Swag 111
48 Break Slips. 113
49 Scratch-Off Lottery Cards 115
50 Social Skill Slam Book 117

Teaching & Learning
51 Doughy Designs. 122
52 Anchor Charts. 125
53 Observation Bottles 128
54 Costumes. 131
55 Off-the-Page Word Walls 133
56 Stick Puppets. 136
57 Surprise Bags. 138
58 Frisbee Toss. 140
59 Pop-Ups. 142
60 "All Done" Board 144

Literacy
61 Page Turners 148
62 Vocabulary Bars 150
63 Building Block Sentences 152
64 Story Stones. 154
65 Slant Board 157
66 Story Starter Sticks. 159
67 Word Exchange. 162
68 Notebook Flipper 164
69 Poetry Dice 166
70 3D-Venn Diagram. 169

Mathematics

71 Foldables 174
72 Interactive Bulletin Boards 176
73 Numbers Alive 178
74 Graph Guides 180
75 Sticky Sticks. 182
76 Cardboard Dominoes 184
77 Recycled Keyboard 186
78 Wipe-Off Flashcards 188
79 Checkerboard Review 190
80 Student-to-Student Tutorials 192

Study & Review

81 Customized Bingo Boards. 196
82 Review Tower 198
83 Fortune Tellers 200
84 Hang-Ups 202
85 "Can You Guess?" Game. 204
86 More-Than-Math Hopscotch 207
87 Memory Caps 210
88 Trading Cards. 212
89 Stackables 215
90 Text Maps 217

Assessment

91   Desktop Displays 220
92   Censograms. 223
93   Visual Rubric. 225
94   Comic Strip Check-In. 227
95   Exit Slip Display 230
96   Tic-Tac-Toe Board. 232
97   Notebooks 235
98   Kiddie Lit Creations. 238
99   Multiple-Choice Fans. 240
100 Teacher Report Cards. 242

Also by Paula Kluth

A is for "All Aboard!"
(coauthor: Victoria Kluth; illustrator: Brad Littlejohn)

"A Land We Can Share": Teaching Literacy to Students with Autism
(coauthor: Kelly Chandler-Olcott)

From Tutor Scripts to Talking Sticks:
100 Ways to Differentiate Instruction in K–12 Inclusive Classrooms
(coauthor: Sheila Danaher)

"Just Give Him the Whale!": 20 Ways to Use Fascinations,
Areas of Expertise, and Strengths to Support Students with Autism
(coauthor: Patrick Schwarz)

Pedro's Whale
(coauthor: Patrick Schwarz; illustrator: Justin Canha)

"You're Going to Love This Kid!": A Professional Development
Package for Teaching Students with Autism in the Inclusive Classroom

"You're Going to Love This Kid!":
Teaching Students with Autism in the Inclusive Classroom, Second Edition

About the Authors

Paula Kluth, Ph.D., is a former special educator who has served as a general education co-teacher, inclusion facilitator, and instructional coach. Her professional interests include differentiating instruction, active learning, and inclusive schooling.

Dr. Kluth is the author or coauthor of eleven books including: *"You're Going to Love This Kid!": Teaching Students with Autism in Inclusive Classrooms, Second Edition*; *"A Land We Can Share": Teaching Literacy to Students with Autism*; and *"Just Give Him the Whale": 20 Ways to Use Fascinations, Areas of Expertise, and Strengths to Support Students with Autism*. Paula is also a director of a documentary film titled *"We Thought You'd Never Ask": Voices of People with Autism*.

Sheila Danaher, M.S.Ed., is a consultant for the Christopher L. & M. Susan Gust Foundation, which is dedicated to supporting all students by creating inclusive school communities. She is a former learning specialist and administrator in the Chicago Public Schools, where she focused on supporting students with autism and differentiating instruction for all students. As a consultant, for the Gust Foundation, Sheila continues her work in the Chicago area by providing teachers with ideas for curricular adaptations, differentiating instruction, and implementing the best strategies for supporting students with disabilities in preschool, elementary, and secondary school settings.

Preface

Both of us are visual learners.

For this reason, we published a book on differentiation that featured a color photograph of each highlighted idea. That book—*From Tutor Scripts to Talking Sticks: 100 Ways to Differentiate Instruction in K–12 Inclusive Classrooms*—contained dozens of ideas and covered ten different areas of need, including behavior, literacy, math, assessment, and organization.

When we told friends, colleagues, and readers about our plans to write a second book filled with ideas for differentiating instruction, most were surprised that we had not shared *all* of our favorite ideas in our first book. To be honest, we never imagined that our book would have a sequel, but after it was released we saw so much interest in these simple teacher-tested strategies and had so many creative educators approach us with additional ideas, a second volume quickly seemed inevitable. We not only wanted to share all of these new ideas we discovered but keep ideas flowing to those educators working hard to create responsive classrooms for all of their students.

One such teacher was described in the preface of our first book. Ms. M. was a middle school teacher we met who insisted that she could not adapt her literacy lessons for students with disabilities. We explained the dozens of strategies she could employ. We brought articles on the latest research in literacy. And we told her stories of how we, as educators, had successfully used the same strategies in our own teaching. None of these approaches seemed to impact her practice.

Then we visited a second time and brought *examples* of our suggestions with us. We brought adapted literature; software that would help all of her students learn faster and more easily; graphic organizers to use with the entire class; and novelty pencils, augmentative communication devices, and dry erase boards to motivate her reluctant writers. She not only used the suggestions immediately but started developing her own materials for diverse learners.

Like our first book, we came to this second project keeping teachers like Ms. M. in mind and believing in the idea that if differentiation is needed for students, it is needed for teachers too. So, for every educator who is also a visual learner, this book is for you!

Acknowledgments

This book and all projects we pursue together would never have come together without Christopher and Susan Gust. Thank you for asking the question, "What is possible?" over and over again.

So many clever educators contributed ideas to this book, including those from St. Benedict High School in Chicago, Illinois, and from Howard County Public Schools in Howard County, Maryland. Individual teachers who have specifically added ideas include Julie Brandolino, Julia Snider, Lindsay Shumaker, and Shannon Brusca. To say "we love your work" is an understatement.

We would also like to thank those who worked so hard to assemble the books such as Nora Sanchez, who served as our project photographer. Nora, we are so sorry that we waited until the last minute to put you to work. Even when you are forced to snap photos at a frantic pace, however, your work is dazzling. Help from Kaitlynn Philbin was, as usual, invaluable. Kaitlynn, you can finally take a break from cutting, pasting, copying, modge podging, and assembling. Jaclyn Beljung not only contributed classroom ideas but provided suggestions for many web sites and vendors. Jacyln, you brought not only much needed elbow grease to the project but beautiful materials and student-centered thinking. We also send our gratitude to the masterful Kate Zagorski. Everything you touch turns into a classroom masterpiece! We also are indebted to Stephanee "ask and you shall receive" Kukankos. Stephanee, what should have taken us days took minutes because of you.

Patrick Schwarz, we admire all you do to support students in inclusive schools. Your work inspires our teaching *and* our writing.

Lots of love to our families—both here and in Florida. Erma and Willa, your input is so appreciated. It is beyond helpful to have both a first-grade expert and a third-grade expert in house. And to Sheila's family and friends we are so grateful for those who helped with the big move back home during our deadline week.

And we are, of course, so grateful to those at Paul H. Brookes Publishing Co. for their investment in this book. Rebecca Lazo was as supportive as ever and never seemed to tire of our often-unintentionally-hilarious rhyming title ideas. Jill Eccher provided just the structure, organization, and eye for detail we needed. And Steve Plocher was the glue that held it (and us) all together. Thank you. Thank you. Thank you.

This one is also for the Gusts.
Thank you for your constant commitment to
schools for all and for reminding us of the power of one.

Organization

Contents

1 Talk-o-Meters 2

2 Lit Bins 5

3 Month-at-a-Glance Calendar 7

4 Clipboard Corral 9

5 Personalized Learning Agenda 11

6 Protocol Book 13

7 Flexible Grouping Tools 16

8 Helping Hand 18

9 Student-Friendly Storage 20

10 Volunteer Ads 23

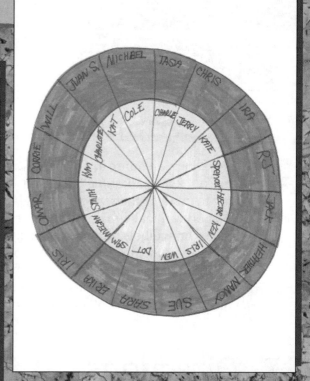

1 Talk-O-Meters

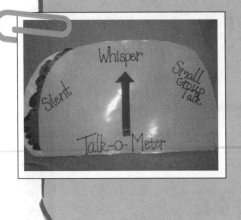

Materials

- Poster board
- Extra piece of cardboard
- Hook and loop tape or thumb tack
- Markers or paint

Description

As teachers use more interactive strategies, their classrooms become busier and often noisier. To manage all of the bustle, educators often turn to visual supports to teach students how to monitor their voices throughout the day.

You can make many different types of meters, as well as incorporate many different images or symbols into your visual. For instance, some teachers use a number scale, with *0* indicating the need for silence, *1* meaning whispers only, and so on. Other teachers use pictures as cues (e.g., a closed mouth means silence, one mouth means quietly talking, two mouths means normal classroom voices, three mouths means group work and multiple voices are okay). Still others may incorporate colors as cues.

Directions

To create your own talk-o-meter, simply use poster board to create your visual and arrow and add hook and loop tape to both the arrow and to the parts of the poster where you will stick the indicator. You can also use a thumb tack to attach your indicator. Lamination will create a longer-lasting visual.

Once your talk-o-meter is constructed, you are ready to put it into use. Begin by posting your meter in a prominent place. Then, move the arrow (or other indicator) throughout the day to help learners see what voice levels they need to maintain during given activities or lessons.

Some teachers use two arrows or indicators: one to show the preferred volume level and one to show the current classroom level. Use the method you feel works best for your student or students.

Examples

In a mixed-age primary classroom, a teaching team used a number scale as part of their talk-o-meter. They labeled the numbers as *no voice* (1), *whisper voice* (2), *indoor voice* (3), and *outside voice* (4). In the absence of the poster, the teachers would hold their fingers up to indicate desired voice levels.

A fifth-grade teacher created a talk-o-meter to help students learn the appropriate voice volume for different classroom structures. Instead of having levels, she used the following labels: *work alone, partner talk, small group/quiet voices,* and *whole-group discussion.*

A speech pathologist created an individual talk-o-meter for a student with Asperger syndrome who struggled to modulate and monitor his own voice. The student's talk-o-meter featured pictures of superheroes because of his love of comic books. His scale showed a superhero with a closed mouth for silence, a superhero cupping his hand around the ear of another hero to indicate "whisper voice," and so on.

One elementary school teacher created a fun visual for her students. She cut her voice monitor board into a tasty-looking shape to create a taco talk-o-meter or "taco-meter"!

Keep in Mind

Talk-o-meters are helpful tools, but they likely will not have much of an impact unless students are explicitly taught how to read and respond to the information. Therefore, you should first set the talk-o-meter and remind students of the expected voice levels before the lesson begins. It is easier to set the tone at the beginning of the lesson than during the lesson when the voices have exceeded an acceptable volume.

Reference

Golon, A. (2008). *Visual-spatial learners.* Waco, TX: Prufrock Press.

Vendor

Dick Blick Art Materials

http://www.dickblick.com

You will find everything you need to make your posters, including poster board, paint, markers, and lettering stencils and stickers.

Web Site

Smart Classroom Management

http://www.smartclassroommanagement.com

Looking for more ideas for creating a productive and comfortable classroom? Check out Michael Linsin's blog for tips on creating classroom procedures, setting rules, and proactively dealing with challenges.

2   Lit Bins

Materials

- Cardboard magazine holders
- Photos of students or student illustrations
- Large classroom library

Description

Differentiating instruction is not only about meeting individual learning needs; it is also about seeing uniqueness in students and using materials that each will find relevant and even compelling. One simple way to achieve this goal in the area of literacy instruction is to create lit bins for every student in your classroom and regularly fill them with recommended reading and related materials.

Some scholars believe that students spend too much time reading selections that have been assigned classroom wide and not enough time selecting and reading titles that match their personal interests. If you have the ability to do so, you can use your bins as a way to lead students into a wider range of titles, subjects, and genres, while still giving them the power to choose what they ultimately read.

Even if you must stick to whole-class book study for most of your lessons, students can take these recommended books home or read them on the bus, before school, or during other free time. By implementing lit bins as a differentiation strategy, you can make sure that students have opportunities to check out books that are appropriate for their ages, interests, and reading levels throughout the year.

Not all of these selected materials need to be related to requirements. You could slip a cartoon relevant to a student's hobby into his bin, or you might share a new magazine that the student can read in his or her free time.

Directions

Ask students to find a book they love either in their desk or from the classroom library. Take a photograph of each individual student holding his or her favorite book. Other variations of this include having students draw a self-portrait to affix or asking them to adorn their bin with their favorite reading selection so all of their classmates (and their teacher) can get a sense of what types of books that person appreciates. This is helpful for making recommendations throughout the year. Once you have decided on how to decorate or label your bins, add an image to each bin.

Put the bins near your classroom library to make filling and pruning of the bins easier. As you fill the bins, keep track of which titles have been "checked out" by which students. Teach students this same process so they can record any recommended titles they return and keep track of any books they check out on their own. You can also encourage students to make recommendations to one another by leaving a stack of *A Book You Might Like* forms in your library. Students can sign their names and write short messages about why they are making the recommendation. The form can then be stuck into the pages of the book before it is filed in a bin.

Example

A middle school teacher maintained 50 lit bins in her small classroom by limiting the number of books in each to two and by assigning different students each week to maintain the space and the materials. The lit bins are one tool that helps her differentiate her literacy instruction, while making personal connections to her learners via her recommendations.

References

Ayers, R., & Crawford, A. (Eds.). (2004). *Great books for high school kids: A teacher's guide to books that can change teens lives.* Boston, MA: Beacon Press.

Gillespie, J.T., & Barr, C. (2004a). *Best books for high school readers: Grades 9–12.* Santa Barbara, CA: Libraries Unlimited.

Gillespie, J.T., & Barr, C. (2004b). *Best books for middle school and junior high readers: Grades 6–9.* Santa Barbara, CA: Libraries Unlimited.

Hinton-Johnson, K., & Dickinson, G. (2005). Guiding young readers to multicultural literature. *Library Media Connection, 23,* 42–45.

Hipple, T., & Claiborne, J.L. (2005). The best young adult novels of all time or *The Chocolate War* one more time. *English Journal, 94,* 3.

Miller, D. (2009). *The book whisperer: Awakening the inner reader in every child.* San Francisco, CA: Wiley.

Vendor

Demco

http://www.demco.com

Get all of your library supply needs met at Demco including cardboard magazine holders.

Web Site

The Book Whisperer

http://www.bookwhisperer.com

The Book Whisperer web site includes resources to help educators inspire and motivate students of all ages. From this page, you can access Donnalyn Miller's blog, Twitter, and Facebook page. Her site also features a regularly updated book recommendation page.

Month-at-a-Glance Calendar

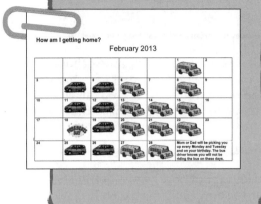

Materials

- Clip art
- Paper

Description

Many students with disabilities—especially those on the autism spectrum—are visual learners who can comprehend rules, information, and steps better when they are presented graphically. Teachers of these visual learners commonly offer supports such as visual schedules and activity schedules. The month-at-a-glance calendar is a similar tool that can be woven into a student's day. This visual support does not provide an answer to the questions "What are we doing this morning?" or "What is happening next?" as other tools do. However, it does give learners a big-picture look at the month, which can be used for planning and emotional preparation.

Directions

Use month-at-a-glance calendars in situations where the student needs information about day-to-day or week-to-week changes. Common uses of month-at-a-glance calendars include communicating the following:

- After-school activities
- Which parent is picking the student up from school
- Vacations and breaks from school
- Appointments (doctors, dentists, therapists)
- Due dates for assignments

Examples

A month-at-a-glance calendar was created for a student who had a lot of anxiety about an upcoming vacation. His teachers made him a visual to answer the question "When is spring break?"

A student with autism helped to make his own month-at-a-glance calendar of after-school activities. He used it both as a comfort and as a planning tool. At the beginning of each month, the student scoured the school's newsletter for information on football games, pep rallies, and concerts. He added images to represent these events to the calendar and used this process as a way to get more involved in school events.

A young student with cognitive disabilities had a lot of anxiety about how he was getting home each day. His teacher create a month-at-a-glance calendar to show him which days his parents would come and which days the bus would pick him up. She also added a graphic for Presidents Day to communicate to him that this was a holiday and, therefore, not a school day.

Reference

Grandin, T. (1995). *Thinking in pictures.* New York, NY: Doubleday.

Vendor

Schkidules

http://www.schkidules.com

Provides visual schedules, magnets, and other supports to communicate "what happens next."

Web Site

Calendar Labs

http://www.calendarlabs.com

Calendar Labs provides free printable calendars that you can use to create your month-at-a-glance visual aids.

4 Clipboard Corral

Materials

- Two to three dozen clipboards
- Plastic or metal tub

Description

There are many ways to differentiate instruction and meet the needs of diverse learners. One of the most underused techniques is changing the classroom environment, and one of the easiest ways to change the classroom environment is to invite students to sit on the floor. This adaptation requires no expensive materials, very little space, and provides learners with the opportunity to make choices. Of course, if you encourage students to sit on the floor, you will need to offer them a writing surface. This is where the clipboard corral comes in handy.

Directions

Find a bin large enough to house one clipboard for every student in your classroom. Number each board and assign one number to each student in the classroom so you can easily track down a missing board.

Introduce students to the clipboards. Stress that learners do not need to use the boards if they want to stay at their desks, but during the course of the days, weeks, and months of a school year, give several opportunities for learners to "sit anywhere" and then ask them to assess their seating choices. Many students do not know much about their learning style or preferences and most have had little or no experience making decisions related to their own instruction. One way to start is with a class meeting focused on workspaces. Have students brainstorm possible places to work and consider the pros and cons of each. Have students think about themselves as learners: "Do you think you work better alone or with others? Do you work better sitting in a chair or in a different position?" Each student should finish the meeting with ideas they want to try for themselves.

Example

Students in a seventh-grade English class were allowed to "sit anywhere" during independent writing activities, including journaling and quick writes. To encourage students to get comfortable and to inspire a change in the classroom environment, students were invited to grab their clipboards and find a place to work.

Reference

Udvari-Solner, A., Villa, R., & Thousand, J. (2005). Access to the general education curriculum for all: The universal design process. In R. Villa & J. Thousand (Eds.), *Creating an inclusive school* (2nd ed.). Alexandria, VA: Association for Supervision and Curriculum Development.

Vendor

Lynmar Clip Boards
http://www.clipboardsdirect.com
Lynmar Clip Boards provides many different styles of clipboards, including some you can customize.

Web Sites

Clutter-Free Classroom
http://clutterfreeclassroom.blogspot.com
This blog is dedicated to creating neat and organized learning spaces.

The Organized Classroom Blog
http://www.theorganizedclassroomblog.com
Get ideas for designing inexpensive learning materials, keeping the classroom tidy, and creating many do-it-yourself organization tools.

5 Personalized Learning Agenda

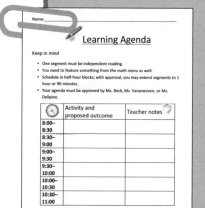

Name:

Learning Agenda

Keep in mind

- One segment must be independent reading.
- You need to feature something from the math menu as well.
- Schedule in half-hour blocks; with approval, you may extend segments to 1 hour or 90 minutes.
- Your agenda must be approved by Ms. Beck, Ms. Vaneveoven, or Ms. Delipino.

⏰	Activity and proposed outcome	Teacher notes
8:00–8:30		
8:30–9:00		
9:00–9:30		
9:30–10:00		
10:00–10:30		
10:30–11:00		

Materials

- Paper
- Schedule template

Description

The field of education has been focused on differentiating instruction for almost 20 years, but methods to truly give students autonomy and individualized learning opportunities are not terribly common. Enter the personalized agenda. This one simple tool consisting of a series of time slots and spaces for adding proposed plans can be used to provide students with permission to set their own goals and choose their own learning activities.

Directions

Decide on when you will use your agendas. Some teachers start with using them for an hour or so each week and then expand to longer periods of time. As you begin to use agendas, be sure that students have clear lists of activities to choose from as well as guidance on how to best spend their time. For instance, students need to know how much of their class requirements have to be finished before they can designate time for an enrichment project, silent reading, or classroom blogging.

Develop a procedure for evaluating student plans. Will you have them submit their agendas for approval? Will you glance at their choices as you circulate during independent work time? How will you assess their progress and productivity? These questions might be answered first at the launch of the format, then revised and updated after you have seen the agendas in action.

Example

All of the students in an eighth-grade English class worked from personalized agendas every Thursday and Friday. The classroom was co-taught both days so teachers could review agendas with learners as they walked through the classroom working with individuals and small groups. Students might be reading independently, writing or editing, conferencing with peers or teachers, completing unfinished classwork, or learning a new skill such as playwriting. Agendas had to be approved by a teacher each week and progress and/or completed work had to be documented.

Reference

Gibbons, M. (2004). Pardon me, didn't I just hear a paradigm shift? *Phi Delta Kappa 85*(6), 461–467.

Vendor

School Mate

http://www.schoolmate.com

School Mate provides agenda books personalized for your school.

Web Site

Self-Directed Learning

http://www.selfdirectedlearning.com

This web site provides resources and information on how to encourage self-direction in the classroom.

6 Protocol Book

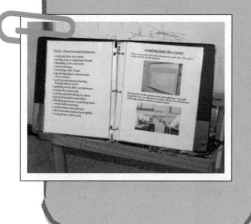

Materials

- Camera, video camera, tablet computer, or phone with camera/video
- Photographs
- Photo album or binder

Description

Teachers often spend the first 6 weeks or so of school teaching their students various classroom routines, such as handing in homework, using the classroom library, changing classes, submitting late assignments, lining up, getting lunch, and finding a book for silent reading. Students learn these routines by practicing them every day, but you can reduce your management time by creating classroom protocol books that feature clear steps for all of your classroom or school routines.

Directions

Take photographs of students following a particular routine and place them in order on a page with some simple instructions. Follow this same strategy for all classroom routines.

Then, create a binder or virtual bulletin board with all of the routines posted. If you use an electronic option for posting, you can also add video to make the expected behaviors even more clear.

Provide time for students to review these materials and ask for help in updating the content when necessary.

Some of the procedures or protocols you might include in your book include the following:

- Lining up
- Coming into the room
- Leaving the room
- Using the assignment book
- Handing in homework
- Helping classmates/peer tutoring

- Working with tablets and interactive white boards
- Participating in classroom discussions
- Getting assistance during independent work
- Getting work after an absence
- Taking breaks/using the restroom
- Eating and drinking in class
- Completing classroom jobs and roles
- Finding partners or getting into cooperative groups
- Using a classroom library
- Getting lunch and cleaning up
- Reacting to fire, tornado, and lockdown drills
- Finishing work and finding an appropriate activity

 # Examples

A first-grade teacher was constantly interrupted during her guided reading lessons by students asking questions regarding their centers, so she made a protocol book. The book contained a picture of the teacher wearing a "do not disturb me" red hat and provided clear instructions for steps students could take when the hat was being worn. It also had two photographs of problem-solving techniques to use if students had questions: one photo of a student asking another student (a designated center leader) and another photograph of the student with a think bubble asking, "Do I need the answer now?" The teacher left this book in the classroom library and students read through classroom protocols—including those created for guided reading—at their leisure.

A high school environmental science teacher created a protocol book to help student volunteers take care of the school garden. The book contained visual directions for watering, planting, and weeding.

 ## Keep in Mind

Some of your students may have a harder time learning classroom rules and guidelines. These learners may appreciate a personal copy of the protocol book so they can study or reference it when needed.

Reference

Wong, H.K., & Wong, R.T. (2001). *How to be an effective teacher: The first days of school.* Mountain View, CA: Harry K. Wong.

Vendor

Staples

http://www.staples.com

At Staples, you can get binders, page protectors, papers, and other materials necessary for your protocol book.

Web Site

Scholastic

http://www.scholastic.com/teachers/article/head-behavior-problems-classroom-procedures

Get ideas for your protocol book by reading this post on 30 classroom procedures to teach.

7 Flexible Grouping Tools

Materials

- Posters or pieces of poster board
- Index cards
- Markers

Description

In diverse classrooms, students are constantly assembled into different groups. Learners are grouped and regrouped based on different goals of lessons. Sometimes educators may group by interests. Other times they may group by abilities. Still other times, they may put students together based on shared goals. Students can also be grouped with others who share their learning styles. Finally, students may be grouped randomly. By using such a wide range of groupings, teachers can be sure that students get opportunities to work with all others in the classroom, have opportunities to build on their strengths and address needs, and not only learn with peers but learn from them.

To make this process a bit easier, some teachers use flexible grouping systems such as decks of cards featuring different pairings and groupings on each card, posters listing various grouping possibilities, or even a movable wheel-type chart that can be turned to reveal ever-changing classroom pairings.

Directions

Before grouping students for any activity, ask yourself the following question: "What is the learning outcome of this activity and what is the best type of grouping to meet this learning outcome?" Then group your students accordingly.

You may want to post your system in the classroom or at least make it available to learners in some way, so they can find their assigned groups or pairs as quickly as possible during an activity.

Examples

Students in a ninth-grade American history class are assigned to four different groups at the beginning of the year: reading groups, discussion groups, exhibition groups, and study partners. Each grouping has a name and each student is assigned to one of those groupings so that learners can easily find their partners for a given activity. For instance, reading groups are named for U.S. Presidents. When the teacher announces that the reading groups are meeting, the Woodrow Wilson group gets together, the Franklin D. Roosevelt group assembles, and so on.

There are five different ways to be grouped in one first-grade classroom. Students might be told to find their reading buddies (a partner with a very similar reading level), reading pals (partners with different reading levels so that one can read to the other if necessary), brainstormers (four students with different levels of readiness/skill), or trios (three students grouped by learning style or interests). The teacher also uses a spinnable wheel with all learners names included to assign partners randomly for certain activities. The inside wheel has half of the learners' names and the outside of the wheel has the other half of the names. Each time the wheel is turned a notch, a new set of partners is revealed. Students enjoy helping with the wheel and guessing who they might be paired with after each turn.

References

Caldwell, J., & Ford, M. (2002). *Where have all the bluebirds gone? How to soar with flexible grouping.* Portsmouth, NH: Heinemann.

Castle, S., Deniz, C., Baker, C.B., & Tortora, M. (2005). Flexible grouping and student learning in a high needs school. *Education and Urban Society, 37*(2), 139–150.

Vendor

Lakeshore Learning

http://products.lakeshorelearning.com

This vendor provides tools for student grouping, including tables and magnetic grouping charts.

Web Site

The Differentiation Destination

http://www.differentiationdestination.com

This teacher blog is filled with resources for the differentiated classroom. Topics covered fairly consistently include grouping and collaborative work. There is a search box on the blog, so you can type in "flexible grouping" to find posts quickly.

8 Helping Hand

Materials

- Pool noodle
- Scissors
- Cards

Description

Many differentiated classrooms are filled with fun interactive games for students to play in pairs or small groups. Students with poor fine motor skills and motor planning may struggle with some of these games if they require the physical manipulation of materials, such as chips or cards.

The helping hand may be used by these students. This handy little holder will make it easier for a student to view his or her cards, sticks, or chips without having too much extra support from another person. The helping hand can be used across many different learning games. It also can be used to learn or illustrate sequences (e.g., parts of a story, eras in history) if you have flashcards or sticky notes to represent the various pieces or steps.

Directions

Cut a section of pool noodle in half (horizontally), cut only the "top" part of the noodle, leaving the bottom of the ring intact.

Place cards, slips of paper, or sticky notes in the slit.

To add to the stability of your helping hand, you may want to shave a bit of foam off the bottom of your noodle as well. This way, it is less likely to tip over once you add your materials.

Examples

Second-grade students played a math card game to learn place value. Students had to shuffle a few cards in their hands and put each card in order as the teacher called out places as in "Put your five in the tens place." Most students just rearranged the cards in their hands to show the number called (e.g., 1,458), but a few students—including one with mild cerebral palsy—used the helping hand to organize their piles.

A third-grade teacher put her students in groups and gave them each a helping hand and some packets of cards. Then, she quizzed them by asking them to put a variety of items in order, such as the life cycle of the butterfly, a particular food chain, and the order of the planets. Students raced to get the correct answers before other groups. When each group felt their sequence was correct, they simply turned their helping hand around to face the teacher.

Reference

Algozzine, B., & Ysseldyke, J.E. (2006). *Teaching students with medical, physical, and multiple disabilities.* Thousand Oaks, CA: Corwin Press.

Vendor

USA Pool Pros
http://www.usapoolpros.com
This vendor offers pool noodles in many colors.

Web Sites

Adapting Creatively
http://adaptingcreatively.blogspot.com
This blog, which was created by the mother of a young woman with Rett syndrome, features posts about do-it-yourself supports, and provides many tips on how to positively support learners with disabilities.

Tots-N-Tech
http://tnt.asu.edu
A few universities joined to create this web site about adaptations and young children. Many easy tutorials can be accessed by educators, therapists, and families.

9 Student-Friendly Storage

Materials

- Bins, crates, shelving
- Stickers or labels
- Markers

Description

Differentiated classrooms have one thing in common: There are a lot of materials to manage! A wide range of reading materials are typically available. There may be many different centers or stations created at different points in the week, and learners may be using different types of technology, including tablets and laptops. These materials can be an unwieldy task for teachers and teaching teams to manage unless they enlist the support of the students to serve as equal partners in the management and organization of their learning spaces.

Many teachers of young children create classroom jobs. In the upper elementary grades, middle school, and high school, this sort of attention to sharing the workload is rarely seen. However, as learners age, they are so much more capable not only of organizing the classroom with and for you but also of proposing new organizing systems that might improve student access to materials.

Many reasons exist for creating student-friendly organizing solutions. All teachers, of course enjoy having a neat space, but orderly classrooms also help students learn responsibility and strategies for organization. In particular, students with learning disabilities, autism, and Asperger syndrome may have organizing objectives on their individualized education programs. Why not address those goals daily by creating well-designed systems that all students can help to maintain?

Directions

Search the Internet and visit other classrooms to find solutions for your particular classroom and the kinds of materials you need to manage. When you discover systems you would like to create, begin shopping for both materials and support.

For your materials, you might be able to look around the school and find items you can upcycle or recycle. Cardboard boxes might make great project bins. Old milk crates could serve as shelving in your library.

Ask for support from colleagues, families, and students. Colleagues might want to help by giving tips on how they solved organizing problems. Some will have a gift in this area and may be excited about providing help to a fellow organizing enthusiast. Parents are great resources in this area, but you may have to be very specific with your request. For instance, let the parents know that you are redesigning your library and need three parents for 3 days in a row to sort books and affix labels. Students—especially those in middle school and high school—are perhaps the best resource of all. They are old enough to work with limited supervision, and some of them may be better at organizing material than you are! Ask them for ideas that are student friendly and find time for them to help you launch and maintain your systems.

Examples

Using colorful bins, small cardboard signs, and a few thousand mailing labels, a new third-grade teacher created a classroom library that became the envy of her colleagues and an easy management job for her 29 students. She created colorful picture labels and titles for each bin (biographies and autobiographies, poetry, science fiction) and then affixed a corresponding label to the top right corner of each book. The label contained the same image and title on the bin. This system could easily be managed by any student in the classroom, including two students with disabilities who were emerging readers and would likely not have been able to make matches with the text alone. Every day, one student was responsible for checking bins to be sure the correct books were in the right bins.

Plastic crates with large numbers filled one closet in the science classroom. Each number represented one science laboratory station. At the beginning of each lab, the teacher put a list of necessary materials on the board. The materials manager (who rotated monthly) went to the closet and retrieved the necessary materials. At the end, the materials manager was also responsible for returning the materials to the correct bin. If students became confused about the mixing of materials during the daily activities, they were able to quickly determine which materials belonged to which bin by looking at the duct tape wrapped around the cords, bases, and necks of laboratory equipment. Each station was also assigned a color, so the teacher could easily see which stations had lost, needed, or misplaced materials. Because the duct tape could be found in each bin, the materials manager was also responsible for asking a team member to tape any equipment pieces in need of new pieces.

Reference

Goldberg, D., & Zwiebel, J. (2005). *The organized student.* New York, NY: Fireside.

Vendor

Lakeshore Learning

http://products.lakeshorelearning.com/search#w=organization

You will find many bins, boxes, shelving systems, and paper-managing tools in this section of the web site.

Web Sites

Get Organized Now

http://www.getorganizednow.com/art-students.html

Browse this site to find many useful tips for organizing any space. Start by reading this post on helping students get organized.

The Organized Classroom

http://www.theorganizedclassroomblog.com

The name of this blog says it all! Subscribe to get ideas for an efficiently run classroom.

TrackClass

http://trackclass.com

This web site provides free organizing tools for students.

10 Volunteer Ads

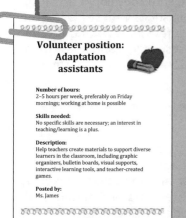

**Volunteer position:
Adaptation
assistants**

Number of hours:
2–5 hours per week, preferably on Friday mornings; working at home is possible

Skills needed:
No specific skills are necessary; an interest in teaching/learning is a plus.

Description:
Help teachers create materials to support diverse learners in the classroom, including graphic organizers, bulletin boards, visual supports, interactive learning tools, and teacher-created games.

Posted by:
Ms. James

Material

- Paper
- Computer

Description

The most underused supports in the differentiated classroom may be human beings. We so often hear that schools do not have the personnel they need to individualize work. However, in many classrooms, few if any volunteers are used, including parents in the school community.

We have talked to teachers about this concern and found that many find volunteers hard to manage. Some educators are unsure of which tasks to give to volunteers. Others are unsure how to secure the right people for the right jobs. To address this concern, we often suggest creating volunteer ads. By crafting an advertisement for a specific role in the classroom, you get volunteers who are very interested in one specific job. In addition, you have already started the process of educating that person on what tasks you need accomplished.

A well-managed group of volunteers can make a huge difference in a differentiated classroom. If you structure your program with care, you can give all students regular opportunities for reading aloud, editing their written products, pursuing individual research, and working on challenging problems and questions with immediate feedback from an adult. You can have help managing students as they work independently while you talk to your students in small groups or one to one. You might also be able to bring expertise and new voices into lessons in the form of local artists, engineers, designers, writers, actors, physicians, and veterans.

Directions

Start reading volunteer ads for other organizations to get ideas for both the roles and the responsibilities you want to feature in your ad.

Then, construct your ad and decide where and how to share it. You might post it on the school web site, in a newsletter, or on a poster in the hallway. If you want to attract volunteers beyond school doors, you may have to use other methods. If you want senior citizens, for instance, call community groups serving that population.

Examples

A group of high school teachers wanted to offer enrichment in the area of creative writing. Because they taught in a community known for the arts, they were sure they could find local writers who would donate time to give minilessons and conduct workshops with students. The teachers wrote a compelling advertisement and shopped it out to a few local writing groups. They had a tremendous response to the ad and landed several guest speakers and a few long-term volunteers who were available to conference with students interested specifically in writing a novel or nonfiction book.

In a kindergarten classroom in a struggling school, two co-teachers knew they needed to spend more time working with individual students during math and literacy centers if they were going to reach their common goal of raising student performance by more than 15% on district assessments. They put out a detailed ad in the school newsletter and attracted 10 weekly volunteers. Two volunteers came each day: one during literacy centers and one during math centers. These volunteers facilitated the activity and answered students' questions while the two teachers worked at centers with either small groups or individual learners.

Reference

Jones, R. (2009). *Turning parents into volunteers.* Valley Stream, NY: Serenity Enterprises.

Vendor

Teachers Pay Teachers

http://www.teacherspayteachers.com/Browse/Search:volunteer

In this amazing collection of resources, you will find volunteer forms, thank-you ideas, and volunteer kits for training and support.

Web Sites

A Mom with a Lesson Plan

http://amomwithalessonplan.com/how-to-volunteer-helping-your-kids-teacher

If you want some ideas for using volunteers who cannot come into the classroom, check out this post and download the printable form.

PTO Today

http://www.ptotoday.com/pto-today-articles/article/8-25-ways-to-catch-and-keep-volunteers

This is a helpful site in general for teachers, but the article on "catching and keeping" volunteers is a must read.

Environment & Sensory

Contents

11   Reading Windows 26

12   Visors 28

13   Relaxation Jars 30

14   Weighted Pencils 33

15   Locker Scribbles 36

16   Salt Maps and Figures 38

17   Weighted Snakes 40

18   Brain Break Bucket 42

19   Worksheet Peek 45

20   Sensory Book Jackets 47

11 Reading Windows

Materials

- Transparent file folder
- Manila file folder
- Tape
- Scissors

Description

The use of colored overlays seems to help some individuals with dyslexia and other reading disabilities improve their functional reading skills. Other students may not have reading disabilities, but may find it helpful to use a simple masking tool to isolate single words, sentences, or rows of sentences—especially during particularly challenging passages. Because individual needs may vary significantly, you will need to work with your student to determine his or her individual preference regarding not only the use of color, but the size of the reading window as well.

Directions

Cut both your transparent file folder and your manila folder into strips that are approximately 2 inches wide.

Fold the manila folder strip in half. Cut a rectangle out of the inside of the manila folder strip by cutting from the closed end of the fold to the open end of the fold. For younger students, you should cut a wider window because the print in their books is larger. Cut smaller windows for older students or for students who are reading at the chapter book level.

Open the manila folder strip. Place a strip of transparency file folder over the cutout you have created.

Place another cut out manila folder strip over the colored transparency to make a "window." Tape the outside edges of the manila folder pieces to make sure the transparency stays inside.

Before distributing the reading windows to students, check with your school or district reading specialist to see if they have specific recommendations for how and when to introduce the windows. Once your students have their overlays, you may also want to collect some informal data to gauge their effectiveness.

References

Scott, L., McWhinnie, H., Taylor, L., Stevenson, N., Irons, P., Lewis E., et al. (2002). Coloured overlays in schools: Orthoptic and optometric findings. *Ophthalmic and Physiological Optics, 22,* 156–165.

Stone, R. (2003). *The light barrier: Understanding the mystery of Irlen syndrome and light-based reading difficulties.* New York, NY: St. Martin's.

Vendors

National Reading Styles Institute

http://store.nrsi.com/nrsi-colored-overlays.html

Shop for assessment kits and a range of colored overlays.

Really Good Stuff

http://www.reallygoodstuff.com/product/irlen+colored+overlays.do

On this web site, you can purchase colored overlay pages.

Web Site

Irlen

http://irlen.com

Helen Irlen is the nation's leading expert in perceptually based reading and learning difficulties. She uses colored overlays and filters to improve the brain's ability to process visual information. Read more about the Irlen method, view and purchase products, and receive additional information on this site.

12   Visors

Materials

- Foam visor
- Markers or puffy paints

Description

Many students on the autism spectrum and others with related needs find classroom lighting (especially fluorescent lighting) overwhelming to their sensory systems. Lighting can be made more tolerable by moving the student away from direct downward projecting lighting, moving him or her closer to natural lighting, incorporating some lamp lighting, or providing the learner with a baseball cap or visor.

Directions

Distribute the foam visors to your students and discuss how they might be used across environments and activities. Then, provide markers, stickers, and paints so that learners can decorate and personalize their visors.

Remind learners to use their visors any time they need a break from direct light, including at recess if necessary.

Example

Lauren, a third-grade student on the autism spectrum wears her visor when she sits at her desk. She takes it off when she is not directly underneath the banks of fluorescent lights.

Keep in Mind

Some students who will not tolerate a visor may be open to wearing another type of head covering, such as a baseball cap.

Reference

Kluth, P. & Shouse, J. (2009). *The autism checklist: A practical reference for parents and teachers.* San Francisco, CA: Jossey-Bass.

Vendors

Party Palooza

http://www.partypalooza.com

Get inexpensive visors in six different colors.

Tennis Express

http://www.tennisexpress.com

Shop this site for higher-quality visors that may be more appropriate for your older students. They also have a huge selection of baseball caps.

Web Site

SPD Blogger Network

http://www.spdbloggernetwork.com

The Sensory Processing Disorder Blogger Network is a community of parents who blog about their children with sensory processing problems. You will not only find teaching tools, but advice and insights from those who live with these issues daily.

3 Relaxation Jars

Materials

- Canning jar, peanut butter jar, or baby food jar
- Glitter glue
- Glitter
- Hot water

Description

Some teachers give their students breaks outside the classroom when they are feeling anxious or frustrated. These breaks can be helpful (and should absolutely be used when necessary), but they may not always be needed if tools are available in the classroom to help students unwind right at their seats. The relaxation jar is one such tool. It can be used classroom-wide or created for individual students to keep in their desks or lockers.

Directions

Pour 1 tablespoon of glitter glue and a cup of hot water into the jar. Depending on the size of your jar, you may need to add a bit more or less of each. Then add the food coloring of your choice and a tiny tub of glitter.

If you have combined the ingredients correctly, it should take about 5 minutes for all the glitter to settle. For many students, this is enough time to relax and regroup.

Example

A fifth-grade teacher offers students opportunities to "chill out" in a classroom safe space when they need a quick break. The space includes headphones, a study carrel to duck behind, and some tabletop tools to help students unwind, such as worry stones and a relaxation jar.

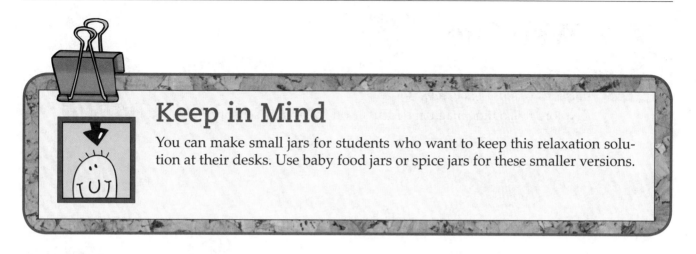

Keep in Mind

You can make small jars for students who want to keep this relaxation solution at their desks. Use baby food jars or spice jars for these smaller versions.

References

Biel, L., & Peske, N. (2009). *Raising a sensory smart child: The definitive handbook for helping your child with sensory processing issues.* New York, NY: Penguin.

Plummer, D.M. (2012). *Focusing and calming games for children: Mindfulness strategies and activities to help children to relax, concentrate and take control.* Philadelphia, PA: Jessica Kingsley.

Shapiro, L., & Sprague, R. (2009). *The relaxation and stress reduction workbook for kids.* Oakland, CA: New Harbinger.

Vendors

The Container Store

http://www.containerstore.com

The Container Store offers dozens of jars and other containers perfect for the creation of unique relaxation jars.

Fun and Function

http://funandfunction.com/groovy-lava-lamp-p-2346.html

Some students may love the colors and shapes of a lava lamp as much if not more than a relaxation jar. This is just one of the sensory supports available on the Fun and Function web site.

Office Playground

http://www.officeplayground.com

This web site offers an impressive selection of desktop relaxation items including dozens of liquid motion toys (e.g., glitter wands, water games).

Web Site

Sensory Flow

http://www.sensoryflow.com

Explore this online magazine focused on "all things sensory."

14 Weighted Pencils

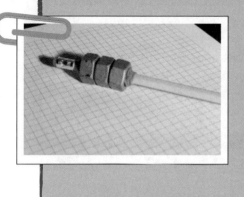

Materials

- Pencils
- Hex nuts
- Rubber bands

Description

Do you have students with fine motor issues? For less than a dollar, you can try this simple technique with any learner who experiences hand fatigue or motor planning problems. For some, weighted pencils can increase writing legibility and build hand strength.

They are appropriate for students of any age. Older students, in fact, may be interested in helping to assemble their pencils and assessing their effectiveness.

Directions

Start by wrapping the rubber band around the pencil, which will prevent the hex nuts from slipping off the pencil during assembly.

Next, place the hex nuts on the pencil to create the desired weight. Wrap another rubber band around the pencil at the end of the hex nuts.

After the student uses the pencil a few times, you can determine if he or she requires more or less weight.

Examples

A high school student with hand tremors made his own weighted pencils to use in classes.

An elementary school art teacher created weighted writing instruments, including markers, crayons, and pencils, for students in her classroom.

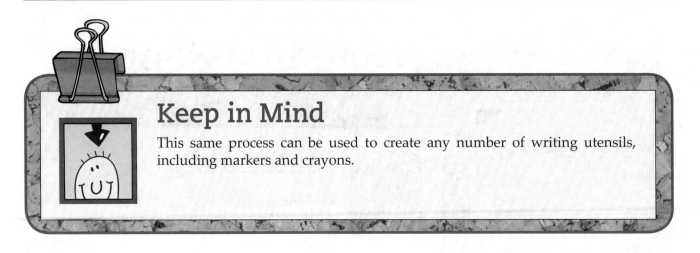

Keep in Mind

This same process can be used to create any number of writing utensils, including markers and crayons.

References

Biel, L., & Peske, N. (2009). *Raising a sensory smart child: The definitive handbook for helping your child with sensory processing issues.* New York, NY: Penguin.

Kurtz, L.A. (2008). *Understanding motor skills in children with dyspraxia, ADHD, autism, and other learning disabilities: A guide to improving coordination.* Philadelphia, PA: Jessica Kingsley.

Sher, B. (2009). *Early intervention games: Fun, joyful ways to develop social and motor skills in children with autism spectrum or sensory processing disorders.* San Francisco, CA: Jossey-Bass.

Vendors

Bulk Office Supply

http://www.bulkofficesupply.com/plasticrubberbands.aspx

Rubber bands can be purchased on this web site in a variety of sizes, quantities, and colors.

Pencils.com

http://www.pencils.com/bulk-pencils

Check out the variety of pencils that can be purchased in bulk. Students may want to try some of the novelty pencils offered such as those that are fuzzy or scented.

Our Creative Minds

http://www.ourcreativemindsinc.com

A pencil with a fidget near the eraser head can be found on this web site. Look in the low-tech tools section.

Southpaw Enterprises

http://southpawenterprises.com/FineMotor/WeightedPencilSet.asp

This weighted pencil set makes it easy to support children who have motor planning problems. The set includes five slide-on weights and a dozen pencils.

Web Site

Therapy Street for Kids

http://www.therapystreetforkids.com

Occupational therapist Mindy Bucker has conveniently organized a resource to support children with fine motor struggles. Strategies are listed for handwriting, meeting sensory needs, and teaching self-help-skills.

15 Locker Scribbles

Materials

- Dry erase single sheets/pages/boards
- Dry erase markers
- Pencil case for each student

Description

Looking for a new engagement or assessment idea that will not only get all students out of their seats, but provide you with almost-instant feedback about what they know and understand? Use locker scribbles to provide every learner with a canvas for solving mental math problems, diagramming science concepts, or illustrating favorite scenes from stories.

This strategy simply involves students traveling to their lockers as a group at various points in your class discussion or lecture. Once they are in front of their own space, they share a response to a question or prompt. You can have students share one quick answer as a way to build in a bit of movement, or you can ask a few questions in a row to keep students out of their seats for a longer period of time. The benefit for the teacher is being able to quickly see the various responses students provide. In this way, locker scribbles serve as both a brain break and a formative assessment.

This "all respond" technique is unique because it allows teachers to see students' responses in a linear format. In addition to using it for individual responses, the class can work together to create timelines, patterns, or interesting graphics.

Directions

Take dry erase pages and mount one on each locker. Encourage students to keep a small pencil case of dry erase markers and an eraser in their lockers to make fast hallway trips easier.

Examples

A fourth-grade teacher mounted dry erase sheets in the hallway outside of her classroom. When her students needed a movement break during her math lesson, she asked them to grab markers and erasers and head to the hallway. The students diagrammed story problems, practiced math facts, and illustrated new vocabulary words.

A sixth-grade teacher used locker scribbles to have students create collaborative products. By assigning each student (or pair of students) one part of a chronology, cycle, or process, the entire class could quickly create a visual support for learning. Students made a timeline of inventions, created a visual retelling of *The Watsons Went to Birmingham*, and wrote π out to 30 places to display it for the school during National Pi Day.

References

Dodge, J. (2009). *25 quick formative assessments for a differentiated classroom: Easy, low-prep assessments that help you pinpoint students' needs and reach all learners.* New York, NY: Scholastic.

Zimmerman, B. (2009). *Pocket doodles for kids.* Layton, UT: Gibbs Smith.

Vendors

Expo

http://www.expomarkers.com

Expo dry erase markers are available in many colors and sizes.

Learning Resources

http://www.learningresources.com

So many teaching materials are available from Learning Resources, including a dry erase coordinate grid boards.

My Visual Display

http://www.myvisualdisplay.com/dry-erase-wall-covering.html

This peel-and-stick dry erase writing surface can be applied to any surface.

Web Site

Busy Teacher

http://busyteacher.org/7082-top-10-ways-to-assess-your-students.html

Although these creative assessment ideas focus on the needs of English-language learners, they can be effective for any student in your classroom.

16 Salt Maps and Figures

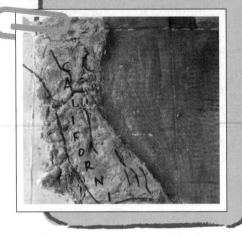

Materials

- Wooden board or thick cardboard
- Flour
- Water
- Salt
- An outline of your image
- Tape
- Pencil
- Permanent marker
- Paint

Description

Many students are tactile learners who have more success in the classroom when they have materials they can feel and physically explore. If students have sensory disabilities, this need is amplified. Students who have low vision, for example, cannot be taught with traditional learning tools like slides/presentations, video, and worksheets. These learners need to have manipulatives, models, and other concrete materials available.

Salt maps are one of the cheapest and easiest ways to meet this need. They can be used at any grade level and by many students at once in a busy classroom.

Directions

Mix flour and salt. Gradually add water, mixing well. If dough is too sticky, add flour. If it is too dry, add water. Unused dough can be stored in the refrigerator in an airtight container for up to a week. The amount of dough needed will vary depending on the type and size of map.

Tape or glue the outline of your image—a map of a country, continent, region, or state—to the cardboard base. Then, cover desired areas with thin layers of dough, using tools to shape the edges as desired.

Place the map in the sun for several hours to dry or simply allow to dry indoors for a longer period of time. Drying time will depend on the thickness of your map.

Paint and label your map.

Examples

A social studies teacher had a learner with low vision. Therefore, he asked students to design salt maps of every region or country the class would study during the year. This project allowed all students to learn about relief maps while unknowingly helping one of their classmates learn tactilely instead of visually.

Social studies and science co-teachers in California had their students create maps of the state. After they were finished, they painted the maps. The students were instructed to include major cities and to add major fault lines as well.

Keep in Mind

Students can use salt and flour to create any number of items. In other words, maps are the most common salt and flour creation, but this recipe can be used to create many different shapes, forms, and figures. Learners might create salt models of animals, triangles, the human heart, cells, story characters, constellations, ancient civilizations, bodies of water, and so forth.

Reference

Forina, R. (2001). *Amazing hands-on map activities.* New York, NY: Scholastic.

Vendors

Raised Relief Maps
http://www.raised-relief-maps.com
No time to play artist? On this web site, you can choose from a variety of state, national park, U.S. region, continent, and world maps.

Utrecht
http://www.utrechtart.com/Modeling-Clay-Sculpture.utrecht
Many different types of modeling clay are available from Utrecht.

Web Site

Perkins School for the Blind
http://www.perkins.org/resources
Visit the Perkins School for the Blind web site to get high-quality lesson ideas and to find links for appropriate materials.

17 Weighted Snakes

Materials

- Long sock or stuffed toy
- Rice
- Needle and thread

Description

Many students need support to stay on-task during long periods of seat work. Weighted "snakes" can offer this support by providing deep-pressure touch and proprioceptive input.

These therapeutic tools can be expensive if purchased, in which case you may only be able to offer these materials to a few students. However, if you make your own "stay put" sensory supports, such as these easy-to-create sock snakes, you can have enough to share with every student in the inclusive classroom.

Directions

Open the sock and pour rice inside, or tear open a long stuffed toy and pour rice into the cavity.

Sew up the sock or toy.

Let your students use their weighted "snake" during any period when they are struggling to stay seated or work.

Example

A third-grade teacher let any of her students use weighted lap snakes during test days or any time they struggled to stay seated or focused. The snakes were kept in a classroom sensory box, which also included desktop fidgets and seat cushions.

References

VandenBerg, N.L. (2001). The use of a weighted vest to increase on-task behavior in children with attention difficulties. *American Journal of Occupational Therapy, 55*(6), 621–628.

Yack, E., Aquilla, P., & Sutton, S. (2002). *Building bridges through sensory integration: Therapy for children with autism and other pervasive developmental disorders* (2nd ed.). Las Vegas, NV: Sensory Resources.

Vendors

Abilitations

http://store.schoolspecialty.com

Choose from two sizes of shoulder snakes on this site.

Dynavox Mayer-Johnson

http://www.mayer-johnson.com/snuggle-snake-washable-unscented

If you do not have the skill or desire to start sewing, you can order the popular "snuggle snake" here.

National Autism Resources

http://www.nationalautismresources.com/glitter-gel-lap-pad-5-pounds.html

Check out this weighted glitter lap pad for the little ones.

Web Site

The Recycling Occupational Therapist

http://recyclingot.blogspot.com

If you want more ideas for do-it-yourself sensory supports, look no further than this OT-created blog filled with art projects and lesson ideas.

18   Brain Break Bucket

Materials

- Small decorative pail
- Tongue depressors or wooden rods
- Marker or stickers

Description

So many students (young and old) crave more movement than they get. However, teachers—especially those in middle school and high school—may feel that they do not have time to incorporate an active learning technique every time they would like to do so. This is when brain breaks come in handy. They are short (usually about 2–3 minutes in length), simple to teach, and provide just enough movement and levity to "reboot" even the most fatigued learner.

To make certain you will remember to incorporate this effective and no-fuss technique on a regular basis, you can create a brain break bucket filled with a range of ideas for increasing blood flow, crossing the midline, and recharging intellectual batteries. To ensure that students don't tire of your breaks, create a fairly large collection of ideas. We suggest starting with at least 30 ideas and adding to your collection throughout the year.

Directions

Find ideas for a series of breaks (or invent them yourself). Print the break ideas on a collection of cards or sticks, with one idea on each. Draw an idea from the bucket and ask students to engage in the break selected. Use your bucket after a long session of sitting, before a test, or when students seem particularly sluggish.

Sample brain breaks include:

- Three-step handshake; repeat 5 times
- Walk and talk with a partner
- Touch all four walls in the room, knock on three tables, and shake hands with two partners
- Twenty-five jumping jacks
- Invisible football toss
- YMCA dance

- Charades
- Chicken dance
- Dry erase doodle time
- Stand and chant (e.g., chant the life cycle of a frog)
- One-song dance party
- Beach ball hot potato
- Indoor hopscotch
- Rock, paper, scissors
- "Air write" the spelling list

Examples

A high school algebra teacher uses a brain break in nearly every one of his 60-minute classes. For example, 20 minutes into the lesson, students might be asked to stand up and walk three laps around the classroom in any direction. After this break, they find a classmate standing nearby and explain a concept, term, or idea that has been covered so far in the hour.

A middle school teacher uses brain breaks in the morning and at the end of the day to energize her seventh graders. Students take turns picking from the bucket every day. Choices include *dance for a minute with music, five-step handshake,* and *beach ball toss.*

References

Jensen, E. (2008). *Super teaching: Over 1000 practical strategies* (4th ed.). Thousand Oaks, CA: Corwin Press.

Scaddan, M.A. (2008). *40 engaging brain-based tools for the classroom.* Thousand Oaks, CA: Corwin Press.

Singh, L., Uijtdewilligen, J.W.R., Twisk, W., van Mechelen, M.J., Chinapaw, M. (2012). Physical activity and performance at school: A systematic review of the literature including a methodological quality assessment. *Archives of Pediatrics and Adolescent Medicine, 166*(1): 49.

Vendors

The Brain Gym Activity Cards

http://www.braingym.com/store-posteraids1.html

These illustrated cards are great for elementary classrooms. You get over 30 cards, including one for each of the Brain Gym activities.

Hasbro Games

http://www.hasbro.com/games/en_US

Hasbro makes a version of Cranium called Brain Breaks, which offers 200 games that can be played in 60 seconds or less.

Web Sites

Brain Breaks

http://brainbreaks.blogspot.com

This is one of the best sites for learning about brain breaks for older students, including those in Grades 9–12.

Jensen Learning

http://www.jlcbrain.com

Eric Jensen is a leading expert on brain-based learning. Visit his professional site and sign up to get his information-packed newsletter.

Differentiation Daily

http://www.differentiationdaily.com

Paula's blog features a new differentiation idea every day during the school year. She regularly features active learning techniques such as brain breaks and collaborative structures.

19 Workshee

Materials

- Manila folder
- Scissors
- Duct tape

Description

"Chunking" assignments into small segments is a common recommendation made to teachers of students with learning disabilities. Methods for chunking include giving out one part of the assignment at a time, formatting written work in a way that allows learners to clearly see separate steps, and even color-coding work in a way that the student understands. Another simple solution involves creating these worksheet peek tools for students to use at home or in the classroom.

Directions

Cut a folder into two or three sections. Demonstrate to the student how he or she can use the adapted folder to block out most of the page and focus only on the section he or she is currently completing. Insert the worksheet or test.

Show the student how to use the folder. Let the student use his or her "peek" during daily work and tests. Provide reminders to do so when necessary.

Example

A middle school teacher had all of her students make their own worksheet peeks to keep in their desks. She told them why and how to use the tools. Students were allowed to use their worksheet peek for any assignment involving written work.

Reference

Riffel, L. (2011) *Positive behavior support at the tertiary level: Red zone strategies.* Thousand Oaks, CA: Corwin Press.

Vendor

Staples

http://www.staples.com

At Staples, you can get manila folders, markers, and all other office supplies in one place.

Web Site

LD Online

http://www.ldonline.org

This web site is one of the best resources available for teacher-tested strategies. You will find other ideas like this one for every grade level.

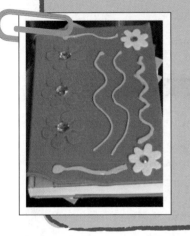

20 Sensory Book Jackets

Materials

- Cloth book jacket
- Hook and loop tape
- Pom-poms
- Puffy paint
- Foam stickers
- Duct tape

Description

Do you have a student who needs desktop fidgets but constantly loses them or forgets to bring them to class? Perhaps you have that learner who gets a bit carried away with handheld objects and they end up flying across the room or bouncing across the floor? If this is true for your students, try attaching fidgets to textbooks. Anything that is somewhat durable and can be easily affixed can work including puffy paints, foam stickers, gem stone embellishments, pom-poms, and decals. Students can either make their own sensory book jackets or you can make them for the few students who need them or for any learner who requests one.

Directions

Place your cloth book jacket on the student's trade book or text book. Then, let the student add the materials that he or she finds the most interesting. You may want to provide models of book jackets that others have created to provide ideas for designs and possible materials. If possible, provide new materials throughout the year to add to the covers or to create new jackets as the materials wear down or come loose.

Be sure to give a bit of guidance on how to "use" the book jacket. Make sure students know, for instance, that the embellishments are meant to be fidgets and that picking or playing with the stickers, jewels, material, and puffy paint is not only okay, but encouraged.

Examples

A fourth-grade teacher offered sensory book covers to a few of her students who were prone to chewing on pencils, carving on desks, and creating their own fidgets from notebook wire and pencil erasers.

A high school student with learning disabilities made her own elaborate and charmingly embellished sensory book covers. They were so remarkable that she ended up creating some for friends who wanted the beautiful and functional creations for their own books.

Keep in Mind

Stuck-on fidgets are not just for books. If book jackets are not commonly used in your school or if you work with students who do not use textbooks regularly, try affixing your materials to the underside of a student's desk. Usually, hook and loop tape is used for this purpose, but you may discover other materials that also work well. To personalize a bit, let students choose different shapes (e.g., strips, circles).

References

Evanski, J. (2009). *Classroom activators: More than 100 ways to energize learners.* Thousand Oaks, CA: Corwin Press.

Martin, L. (2009). *Strategies for teaching students with learning disabilities.* Thousand Oaks, CA: Corwin Press.

Vendors

Office Playground

http://www.officeplayground.com/Fidget-Toys-C102.aspx

Office Playground offers fidget toys for all ages.

U.S. School Supply

http://www.usschoolsupply.com/product/Stretchable_Book_Covers/Book_Covers

Stretchable book covers are available in a variety of colors.

Web Site

Sensory Flow

http://www.sensoryflow.com

Explore this online magazine focused on "all things sensory."

Technology

Contents

21 Book Trailers. 50

22 Word Clouds. 53

23 Community Communicators 55

24 Published Products. 58

25 Projected Directions. 60

26 Class and Student Blogs. 62

27 5-Minute Stylus 64

28 Talking Frame. 66

29 Tap Light Indicator. 68

30 Tablet Prop. 70

21 Book Trailers

My Book Trailer - Goddess Girls

Materials

- Computer
- Video camera
- Online progams such as Animoto.com

Description

Teachers are constantly looking for ways to get their students hooked on reading. Many young readers, however, are spending less time with books and more time on Facebook, web sites, and YouTube. It makes sense, then, to meet students "where they live" and ask them to create electronic alternatives to the traditional book report.

A trailer is a video advertisement for a book. It allows learners to use multiple literacies and to move from the book to the screen and back again in a novel way. Book trailers are modeled after movie trailers and tend to incorporate the same techniques and devices from are seen in cinema previews. Some trailers use just text, music, and images. Others use actors to illustrate scenes or images found in the book. Trailers are qualitatively different from author interviews or readings in that the purpose of the footage is to showcase and interpret the text, not just share the words themselves.

Many educators like using trailers to engage reluctant readers. This assignment not only allows students to work on new skills, such as storyboarding or movie editing, but it results in the creation of tools that can create connections between students and build interest in new reading selections. Therefore, you may find that even the most struggling students enjoy writing or creating this product and are interested in the trailers put forward by their classmates.

Directions

Before you ask students to create book trailers, show them several trailers in the context of your instruction. Use both movie and book trailers so learners can compare the content and the techniques used. Have students pay attention to the uses of actors, text, and music.

Following this exploration, ask students to select a book to advertise. Then, ask them to brainstorm ideas on paper before starting their video product. Have the students jot down a few notes about the trailer, such as the following:

- The beginning or hook
- Use of text, quotes, and passages
- Music
- Special effects
- Length of the video

Finally, have students use tools of their choice to create and edit the book trailers. Students should share with peers midway through the process to be sure their message is clear and essential elements are included.

Example

A social studies teacher asked her students to create trailers of the biographies of historical figures they read for her class. The finished products were shown regularly in class and were available to students in all of her classes who were "shopping" for something new to read.

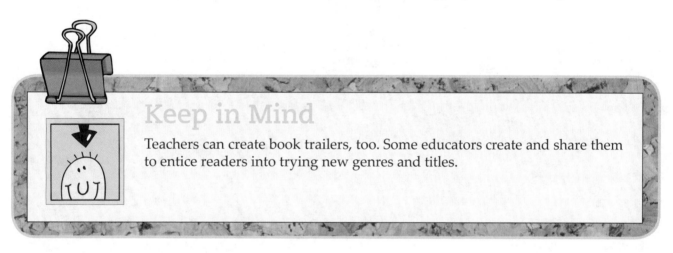

Keep in Mind

Teachers can create book trailers, too. Some educators create and share them to entice readers into trying new genres and titles.

References

Gunter, G., & Kenny, R. (2008). Digital booktalk: Digital media for reluctant readers. *Contemporary Issues in Technology and Teacher Education, 8*(1), 84–99.

Kajder, S. (2008). The book trailer: Engaging teens through technologies. *Education Leadership, 65,* 6.

Vendor

Animoto

http://animoto.com

Animoto makes it possible to quickly create a video using still images, music, video clips, and text. Animoto's free service limits you to 30-second videos. If you want to create longer videos and have more options, you can apply for an education account.

Web Site

Book Trailers for All

http://booktrailersforall.com

This web site was created as a way for people to share their self-created book trailers. Most trailers were created by teachers, students, or librarians, but a number of them were created by publishers or authors.

22 Word Clouds

Materials

- Paper
- Computer/access to Internet

Description

A word cloud is a visual representation of word frequency in a particular passage. The words that appear most often in the text show up in larger sizes than those appearing less frequently, so learners can easily see which words and themes are most relevant or at least repeated in a particular passage, section, chapter, speech, or book.

Directions

Decide on how you want to use word clouds in the classroom. Examples include the following:

- Create a word cloud of a chapter you will be studying next. Ask students to make predictions about the content, the key learnings, the activities, or the assignments.
- Have students share the themes of a chapter or speech they have just read. Then, put the text into a word cloud and have them compare the ideas they shared with the words that show up in the cloud.
- Have students write one-page autobiographies and feed them into word clouds. Then, have students guess which clouds belong to which students.
- Create word cloud poems.
- Create a test review and define all the concepts in the cloud.

Choose the passage, set of responses, chapter, or other text that will be used to generate the word cloud. Type or paste the text into the designated area on the selected web site. Use the tools available on the site to change your word cloud if you want different fonts, layouts, or color schemes.

Examples

During an election year, a high school social studies teacher had his students predict what issues and ideas would dominate each presidential debate. After the debate, he would create a word cloud to compare student predictions with the actual content of the discussion. He also previewed famous speeches the class studied, such as John F. Kennedy's 1961 inaugural address, using word clouds.

On the first day of school, a group of third graders created a word cloud representing their classroom beliefs, norms, and expectations. After a discussion about respect, kindness, and how to create a strong classroom community, every student submitted a few sentences about the kind of learning environment they wanted. Using all of these submissions, the teacher created a word cloud that served as a visual reminder throughout the year of their expectations and hopes for the group and for each other.

References

Johnson, L. (2012). *Kick-start your class: Academic icebreakers to engage students.* San Francisco, CA: Jossey-Bass.

Mirtschin, A. (2010). *Cool tools for the connected classroom.* Melbourne, Australia: Education Services Australia.

Vendor

Zazzle

http://www.zazzle.com/wordle+gifts

Zazzle sells many different word cloud products including posters, key chains, stickers, cups, pins, shirts, and mouse pads. Browse and get inspired.

Web Sites

Tagxedo

http://www.tagxedo.com

Tagxedo turns articles, speeches, themes, letters, poems, and chapters into word clouds. On this site, users can also select a shape for their cloud (e.g., heart, star).

Wordle

http://www.wordle.net

Wordle is one of the most popular cloud-generating sites.

23 Community Communicators

Materials

- One-message communication buttons
- Tape
- Image, symbol, and/or word labels

Description

Communication buttons are usually given to students with disabilities to encourage communication and socialization. By designing a set related to a particular lesson or curricular area, all learners can collaborate and learn a bit about augmentative and alternative communication (AAC).

Buttons can be used for a number of activities, including the following:

- Reader's theater
- Poetry and poems for two voices
- Jokes and riddles
- Fact practice
- Loop games
- Self-correcting quizzes

Directions

Look for opportunities throughout the school day where students with and without disabilities could interact with these AAC devices in the context of a lesson. Choose activities in which one student or various students would have meaningful opportunities to use the same one-message response repeatedly.

Once you have decided on the content, simply tape a small visual to the top of each communicator that will be used in the lesson. If you know that you will keep using your communicator repeatedly for the same purpose, you instead may choose to write or draw on it directly with a permanent marker.

Students may need time to learn how to use their communicators as a group, so do some modeling and give plenty of opportunities to practice.

Examples

Students in an 11th-grade psychology class played a loop game on the anatomy of the human brain. Because one student in the classroom needed to use AAC to play, a few students used community communicators in the game. One student with communication disabilities started the game by asking the question, "Who has the part of the brain important for language comprehension?" Another student used a button to answer, "I have Wernicke's area. Who has the two types of nervous system cells?" and so on.

Students in a ninth-grade English classroom were required to memorize three poems during the year. They could choose any three poems from a class list. To make the task easier and more fun, one small group of learners chose "A Dream Deferred" by Langston Hughes and practiced together using community communicators. Someone always started with "What happens to a dream deferred?" and another team member, usually one of the learners with a cognitive disability, ended with "Or does it explode?"

A teacher at a small Catholic school used community communicators regularly in her Christmas concert. During a performance of *The 12 Days of Christmas*, 12 different students—some with disabilities but most without disabilities—used 12 different buttons to introduce their assigned day in the song. So, the first time *five golden rings* was heard, it was introduced via AAC. On subsequent mentions of that gift, the button was used again, but students also joined in to sing. A young man with cognitive disabilities was responsible for *and a partridge in a pear tree*, so all students were silent to allow this part of the song to be "sung" only by him.

References

Jorgensen, C., McSheehan, M., & Sonnenmeier, R. (2010). *The beyond access model: Promoting membership, participation, and learning for students with disabilities in the general education classroom.* Baltimore, MD: Paul H. Brookes Publishing Co.

Sonnenmeier, R., McSheehan, M., & Jorgensen, C. (2005). A case study of team supports for a student with autism's communication and engagement within the general education curriculum: Preliminary report of the Beyond Access Model. *Augmentative and Alternative Communication, 21*(2), 101–115.

Vendor

Learning Resources
http://www.learningresources.com/search.do?query=communication+buttons
Shop for one-message communication buttons in several sizes.

Web Site

Simplified Technology

http://www.lburkhart.com

Easy ideas for adapted assistive technology and AAC are available on Linda Burkhart's professional site.

24

Published Products

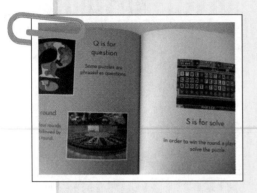

Materials

- Photos or illustrations
- Desktop or online publishing program

Description

To motivate students and make reading material irresistible, some teachers publish books that either students write or teachers create for them. These products can seem more realistic to students and may even provide them with a sense of pride in their work once they see that they have officially "been published."

These books are often used to incorporate the special interests of students on the autism spectrum into literacy lessons, but there are endless other ways to use the books to differentiate instruction and motivate students.

Directions

Create your book with one of the available desktop or online publishing programs. Be sure to decide on the best format for your students. Most companies offer softcover and hard-cover formats in a variety of sizes.

If you want the students to create their own book, have them take or find photographs to use. Student drawings can also be used as illustrations. Scan these images into the computer and upload to the program.

Next, you will need to create the text. The student may want to write or dictate the text, or the teacher can create the story or record the information. As the text is constructed, consider adding or suggesting the addition of new vocabulary or spelling words to support the students in learning new material while they enjoy their new book.

Be sure to pay attention to the size of the font used, especially if a targeted learner has low vision. Pictures should also be sized to meet the needs of individual learners.

Examples

A series of published alphabet books were created for a young man with autism. Because one of his fascinations was game shows, his teachers decided to create a series of books that he would find delightful. His favorite books were embellished over time as a response to his growing reading skills. The first books, therefore, featured only short phrases. Later versions included longer paragraphs and more photos and illustrations.

To interest a young student with multiple disabilities in independent reading, her teachers created a series of language experience stories with and for her. Some of the photos and content were taken from her home life. Other content was related to classroom experiences, such as conducting science experiments, exploring new equipment on the playground, and playing with the class frog.

Reference

Labbo, L.D., Love, M.S., Prior, M.P., Hubbard, B.P., & Ryan, T. (2006). *Literature links: Thematic units linking read-alouds and computer activities.* Newark, DE: International Reading Association.

Vendors

Shutterfly
http://www.shutterfly.com
This personal publishing service can be used by teachers or students to create hardcover or softcover books.

Student Treasures
http://www.studenttreasures.com
On this publishing site, teachers will find lesson plans and sample books.

Web Site

That Writing Lady
http://thatwritinglady.com
Blogger/teacher Catherine Killingsworth has tips on motivation, curriculum, and instruction.

25 Projected Directions

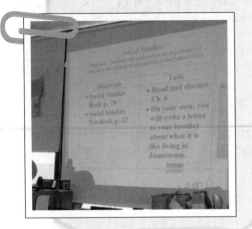

Materials

- LCD projector/computer, interactive whiteboard, or overhead projector (i.e. Smart Board)

Description

Most educators know the value of using visuals in the classroom and while it is common to see them used in the context of daily instruction, it is more rare to see these supports utilized as a classroom management solution and indirect communication strategy. Projected directions are one way to use a visual support to teach skills like literacy, self-management, and organization while helping the classroom to run as smoothly as possible. To implement this idea, type out the verbal directions you provide each day and keep them up long enough to give every learner time to see them and process the information.

Directions

Project directions or a message during any time of the day when there is either a lot of information to share or students need to remember multi-step directions. The best times, then, might be when students enter the classroom, transition to new activities, work in groups, engage in a complex routine, or prepare to leave.

If you are a teacher of students learning English, you might feature directions in two languages, if possible.

Examples

In a kindergarten classroom, the teacher displayed the entrance routine using clip art and words on her interactive whiteboard. The students were able to follow the routine without needing adult cues and reminders, giving students opportunities to be independent and freeing her to start her morning tasks such as lunch count and folder checks.

In one middle school, the procedures for all science labs were displayed. Students could easily see which materials they needed, which steps to follow, and which questions to answer.

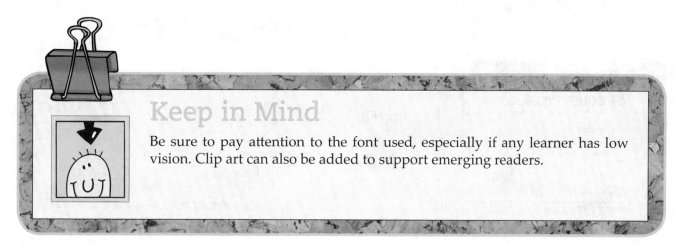

Keep in Mind

Be sure to pay attention to the font used, especially if any learner has low vision. Clip art can also be added to support emerging readers.

Reference

Kluth, P. (2011). "You're going to love this kid!" A professional development package for teaching students with autism in the inclusive classroom [DVD]. Baltimore, MD: Paul H. Brookes.

Vendor

SMART Technologies
http://smarttech.com
This vendor offers interactive whiteboards for the classroom.

Web Site

Amy Laurent
http://www.amy-laurent.com
Amy Laurent's site is filled with visual supports for students with autism and related needs. She posts a new video every month of a unique idea.

26 Class and Student Blogs

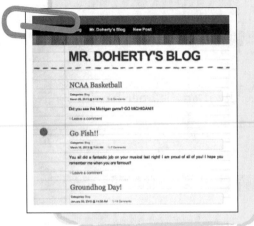

Mr. Doherty's Blog   New Post

MR. DOHERTY'S BLOG

NCAA Basketball

Did you see the Michigan game? GO MICHIGAN!!

Leave a comment

Go Fish!!

You all did a fantastic job on your musical last night! I am proud of all of you! I hope you remember me when you are famous!!

Leave a comment

Groundhog Day!

Materials

- Computer
- Internet access

Description

Blogs are not only a great way for teachers to share information and learn from one another, but they are a unique tool for encouraging communication, writing, and reading. Students who are less than motivated about writing often show interest in communicating with an authentic audience and receiving feedback from readers far and away.

A classroom blog may exist for many reasons. It might be used for sharing student work, connecting to the world beyond the classroom, or learning about digital citizenship. Student blogs can also be used in the classroom. Individuals might create blogs to explore and share a fascination or interest (e.g., lost treasure, the Olympics, horses), engage in a long-term project, reach a goal (e.g., reading 100 books), or get feedback on work (e.g., poetry, art, math challenges, puzzles).

Directions

Choose an appropriate blogging platform. Talk to the technology support teachers in your district about which one is the best for your students, their ages, and your purposes.

Let your administrators and families know what you are doing and clearly share your objectives and your plans for use. Both groups may be concerned about privacy, safety, and how and when the blog will be used. Some may feel the blog will cut into class time or get in the way of "real" work. These types of concerns must be addressed.

After you are ready to begin, set rules for your students. They will need to be aware of issues such as copyright infringement and cyber-bullying.

Finally, choose when and how your learners will blog. Will it be a center or a station that all students access in the classroom regularly? Will it always occur during your language arts block or will students be allowed to write across the school day? Will you rotate the job of head blogger or assign roles for longer segments of time?

Examples

A sixth-grade class started blogging primarily to share their favorite books. Students wrote reviews, fan fiction, and recommendations for their readers. Eventually they shared other writing as well. The blog was a motivating way to engage all students in the inclusive classroom, but it was especially helpful for a student with multiple disabilities who needed extra practice in writing, keyboarding, and communication skills.

An art class blog in one high school was developed to allow learners to showcase their work beyond the classroom. The blog also gave students rich opportunities to dialogue about ideas related to the world of art and their own projects.

Reference

Richardson, W. (2009). *Blogs, wikis, podcasts and other powerful web tools for classrooms.* Thousand Oaks, CA: Corwin Press.

Vendor

Edublogs

http://edublogs.org

Edublogs is a blogging platform made just for educators. There is a free version, but for just a few dollars a month, you can rid your site of ads.

Web Sites

Blogging Through the Fourth Dimension

http://www.pernilleripp.com/2011/05/14-steps-to-meaningful-student-blogging.html

If you are new to blogging and need advice on getting started, you can find plenty of support here.

The Edublogger

http://theedublogger.com

Brought to you by Edublogs, Edublogger was created to share tricks and tips to help the educational blogging community.

Kidblog

http://www.kidblog.org

This web site provides blogging software for students and classrooms.

27   5-Minute Stylus

Materials

- Sponge
- Paper clip
- Duct tape
- A metal pen with a large opening in the tip

Description

Tablets are exploding in popularity in K-12 schools. Teachers are using them to differentiate instruction, and allow individual learners to address different skills in the same lesson. They are also using them to support communication and learning differences. Most students can access tablets by swiping, dragging, and dropping with their fingers, but some users can only be successful when they use a stylus pen. However, the cost of pens may be prohibitive for the classroom. One solution is to make your own stylus with a little wire, a sponge, and an ink pen.

Directions

Remove the cap from the pen body, then remove the ink container and pen nib. Keep the pen cap and body in two separate pieces to make the reassembly easier.

Cut a half-inch square section off the sponge. Cut away any rough scrubbing material to leave just the sponge part.

Straighten the paper clip, leaving just one bend. Place the sponge in the middle of the bend in the paper clip. Use pliers to firmly close the bend to clamp the wire around the sponge.

Drill a hole in the pen body approximately a half-inch from the writing end of the pen. The hole should be slightly larger than the diameter of the paper clip.

Carefully feed the straightened end of the paper clip through the pen cap, into the body of the pen, and out through the drilled hole. Feed the remaining length of paper clip through the hole and insert the cap into the pen body.

Use the pliers to gently push the bent end of the paper clip firmly into the end of the cap to minimize the amount of wire protruding out of the pen.

Grasp the section of the paper clip protruding through the drilled hole with the pliers. While holding the pliers, rotate the pen so the paper clip winds itself around the pen body.

Use a piece of duct tape to cover the end of the wire wrapped around the pen body (cover as little of the paper clip as possible to maximize the conductive surface).

Use scissors to trim the sponge to the desired size.

Be sure that part of the student's hand is touching the wire as he or she is using the pen.

Example

A high school student with cerebral palsy uses an iPad across subject areas. Because of his physical disabilities, it is hard for him to manage a lot of classroom materials and transport them from room to room. The student has a high-quality stylus that he uses for work at home, but he uses teacher-created pens at school. He keeps one in every classroom and a few in his locker.

References

Beukelman, D., & Mirenda, P. (2012). *Augmentative and alternative communication: Management of severe communication disorders in children and adults* (4th ed.). Baltimore, MD: Paul H. Brookes Publishing Co.

Brady, L.J. (2011). *Apps for autism: A must-have resource for the special needs community.* Arlington, TX: Future Horizons.

Scherer, M.J. (2012). *Assistive technologies and other supports for people with brain impairment.* New York, NY: Springer.

Subramanian, C. (2012). *New study finds iPads in the classroom boost test scores.* Retrieved January 30, 2013, from http://techland.time.com/2012/02/22/new-study-finds-ipads-in-the-classroom-boost-test-scores

Vendors

Best Buy
http://www.bestbuy.com
Best Buy carries a variety of stylus pens.

Stylus Shop
http://www.stylusshop.com
A huge selection of pens are available.

Web Site

iLearn Technology
http://ilearntechnology.com
You will find a similar tutorial for a do-it-yourself stylus on this resource-packed site filled with tech-related advice, insights and ideas.

28 Talking Frame

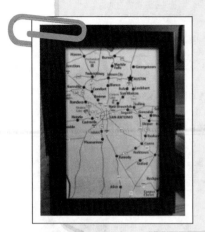

Materials

- Recordable picture frame
- Images related to class content

Description

One of the best ways to help students with disabilities learn new skills related to augmentative and alternative communication and assistive technology is to provide opportunities for all learners to access alternative methods of communication, learning, and interacting throughout the school day.

The talking picture frame is one such tool that all students can access for learning and for a bit of fun. Typically talking picture frames are used by families to record messages related to personal photos, but they can be used in the classroom to "broadcast" fun facts, vocabulary words, potential test questions, or even content-related trivia.

Directions

Choose content for your frame that all students might find interesting or helpful. Then locate an image related to the content, find any recordable frame, and place the image inside the frame. Finally, follow the product instructions to store a message. You might record the message "about 90 percent of an iceberg is under water" and put a photo of an iceberg in the frame. The following day you could keep the photo but change the message to "icebergs are comprised of fresh water."

Depending on the physical and learning needs of your students, you may need to demonstrate how to access the recording. You will also want to set up a routine or ritual involving the frame to be sure that students find opportunities to use it.

Examples

A student with multiple disabilities in a seventh-grade science class had a goal of independently accessing AAC on his individualized education program. He had a formal communication system he used for daily work, but his science teacher helped his goal along by incorporating a talking frame activity daily. The first thing the students did upon entering the classroom was push the button on the frame that was positioned near the classroom door. The frame changed almost daily and might contain any number of facts or ideas about science. For example, one day the picture was a hummingbird; upon hitting the button, students learned that "individuals from some species of hummingbirds weigh less than a penny." Occasionally, the teacher would begin his presentation by finding out who knew the "fact in the frame." The first student who could answer successfully might win a homework pass, granola bar, or pencil.

A social studies teacher used a talking frame to reinforce learning standards and to share related trivia. He changed the frame weekly and asked students to do the recordings of messages such as "Austin is the capital of Texas" and "The Alamo was built by the Spanish Empire in 1744." This gave several of his students who were English language learners a playful way to communicate and use content-area vocabulary. It also gave all students opportunities to hear and learn key information repeatedly as he often used phrases and content more than once.

Reference

Cennamo, K.S., Ross, J.D., & Ertmer, P.A. (2010). *Technology integration for meaningful classroom use: A standards-based approach.* Belmont, CA: Wadsworth.

Vendor

Attainment Family

http://www.attainmentfamily.com/gtone

The GoTalk One is essentially a talking frame with a very large *Play* button.

Web Sites

Assistive Technology Blog

http://bdmtech.blogspot.com

This blog discusses assistive technology for people with reading disabilities, low vision, blindness, and other disabilities.

No Limits to Learning

http://nolimitstolearning.blogspot.com

Subscribe for great commonsense ideas on using assistive technology in learning and in play.

29 Tap Light Indicator

Materials

- Tap light
- Permanent marker

Description

Students who use low-tech communication systems often need a lot of support from a paraprofessional or peer to participate in lessons. If they do not have a support person nearby, there is no way to indicate "I have an idea" or "I want to say something" during a whole-class discussion or lecture. Some students, of course, can raise their hands, but many do not have the strength or range of motion to do so. For these students, a tap light can let the teacher know, "I have something to share." Like hand raising, this support is silent, so it does not disrupt the class. It also can be liberating because students do not need to work through a third party to interact with the teacher.

Directions

Using the permanent marker, write "I have something to share" or a related message on the tap light. You might also draw or affix a picture of a hand on the light to help the student quickly learn the purpose of the device.

To teach the use of the lights, try giving them to more than one student so the learner with a disability can see how others use them to indicate readiness to participate.

Example

A student with multiple disabilities used a tap light to indicate "I have an answer" during class discussions. The teacher taught the use of the light by setting him up to answer very straight-forward questions during lessons. For example, the teacher asked the class to share some of their favorite books. Before the lesson started, a teacher had put a few favorite books on the student's desktop. When she asked the question, a peer prompted the student to tap his light. The teacher called on the young man immediately and he was able to point to one of the books on his desk to answer her question.

Reference

Downing, J.E. (2005). *Teaching communication skills to students with severe disabilities* (2nd ed.). Baltimore, MD: Paul H. Brookes Publishing Co.

Vendors

Home Depot

http://www.homedepot.com

Home Depot offers many different types and brands of tap lights.

Solutions

http://www.solutions.com/jump.jsp?itemType=PRODUCT&RS=1&itemID=16053

Shop for Superbrite touch lights here.

Web Sites

Second Grade Shenanigans

http://imbloghoppin.blogspot.com/2011/09/light-up-your-phonics-instruction.html

This post from a second-grade classroom blog features a clever way to use tap lights to teach spelling.

Speech Time Fun

http://speechtimefun.blogspot.com/2012/03/tap-light-listening-for-sequences.html

Even if you are not a speech pathologist, you may be interested in the many suggestions from this clever professional. This link will take you to an activity that uses tap lights to help students learn and remember sequences.

30   Tablet Prop

Materials

- 1-inch polyvinyl chloride (PVC) pipe, 48 inches in length (depending on the size you wish to make)
- 90-degree, 1-inch PVC elbow, 6 pieces
- 1-inch PVC T-joint, 2 pieces

Description

Some of the best classroom supports are the most basic. To meet the needs of students with physical disabilities and those with fine motor struggles, you can create these simple tablet props out of PVC pipe. They can also be used to prop up textbooks or hold worksheets and packets.

Directions

Cut two 1-inch sections from the PVC pipe. Attach an elbow to each side of the 1-inch sections so that the elbow openings are pointed in the same direction to make a U shape (page holders in the front).

Cut three equal size sections of pipe, 8–12 inches long, depending on the desired height. Using two of these pipe sections, attach one elbow to each piece. Attach each of these pieces to the U-shaped piece created in the first step. Attach the third section of pipe to the upright hole of one of the T joints (this will become the kickstand at the back).

Cut two 3-inch sections of pipe. Attach to each side of the crossbar section of the remaining T joint. Attach each part made in the previous step to each side of the 3-inch pipe section extending from the assembly made in the previous step. Attach the open end of the pipe assembly made in the previous step to the last opening of the T joint assembly (attaching the kickstand to the main frame of the holder).

PVC cement can be used to connect the pieces, or you can leave all parts hand-fitted. Many educators prefer to leave the parts hand-fitted to allow some movement of the assembly to accommodate different materials such as electronic tablets, notebooks, textbooks, and so on.

Example

A special education teacher created many do-it-yourself adaptations for any high school teacher who requested items to support the inclusion of learners with disabilities. Many of these supports were displayed in the teachers' lunch room so that educators could "shop" for items they believed would help students in their classes. Book props were often requested for learners with physical disabilities or fine motor problems.

Reference

Aitken, J.E., Pedego, J., & Carlson J.K. (2012). *Communication technology for students in special education and gifted programs.* Hershey, PA: IGI Global.

Vendors

Active Forever
http://www.activeforever.com/search.aspx?searchterm=book+holder
This vendor offers a variety of book holders.

Maxi Aids
http://www.maxiaids.com/store/prodList.asp
Shop for book holders and many other types of assistive technologies on this site.

Web Site

EdTech Solutions
http://teachingeverystudent.blogspot.com
Great high-tech and low-tech solutions for students of all ages are featured on this blog.

Communication & Participation

Contents

31	Speech Bubble	74
32	Handheld Directions	77
33	"Your Turn" Sharing Stick	79
34	Graffiti Table	81
35	Magnetic Poetry.	84
36	Dialogue Journals	86
37	Reading Phones	89
38	Quick Quip Keychains	91
39	Communication Kits	93
40	Rotating Reader.	95

31 Speech Bubble

Materials

- Poster board
- Wooden dowel or a ruler

Description

Do you have a lot of visual learners in your classroom? If so, you may be interested in incorporating portable speech bubbles into your lectures, whole-class discussions, or presentations. Speech bubbles can serve as visual cues to reinforce ideas, words, or concepts. They also can be used to help communicate the difference between thoughts and or to simply add a bit of humor or whimsy to a lesson.

Directions

To make the speech bubbles, simply cut different shapes or forms out of poster board. To use repeatedly, laminate the bubbles to create a dry erase surface. Then, attach each to a wooden ruler or dowel.

The speech bubbles can be used in many different ways. For example, you can hold up a speech or thought bubble in the following situations:

- To indicate when a character in a book is thinking something vs. saying something
- To indicate that you, as the teacher, are thinking about something (as opposed to reading it or seeing it in the text), which can work especially well during a think-aloud
- To use with a certain catch phrase or key concept at different points during a lecture to provide both visual and auditory input
- To use with a certain catch phrase or key concept to indicate that you want students to chant or repeat that point
- To teach a social skill or study skill (e.g., showing students how you might be upset on the inside but are acting calmly on the outside)

Speech bubbles can be used in skits as well. In fact, you can create human comic strips by having groups of students write scenes related to content and photograph "frames" that include the use of speech and/or thought bubbles.

Examples

A kindergarten teacher uses a speech bubble outside her classroom door. She posts her photo in the hallway and changes the speech bubble message daily. This way, her young learners are motivated to read "the bubble talk" and they can clearly see that the message is a request or message from their teacher.

A sixth-grade teacher in a co-taught classroom uses bubbles to teach students metacognitive strategies, such as reflection and self-assessment. He holds thought bubbles over his co-teacher's head as she is talking about the requirements for upcoming projects. As she acts the part of a student brainstorming project topics, her co-teacher holds up thought bubble questions such as, "What are the smaller tasks within this larger project idea?" "Who could I work with on this project?" and "What would I learn from choosing this project?"

One classroom of first graders gets to use speech bubbles across lessons to share their learnings, ideas, and favorites with classmates. Students regularly parade around the classroom at the end of the day holding their speech bubbles. Their bubbles might be filled with an idea they learned that day, a math fact they mastered, a book they have finished, or a word they discovered.

Reference

Gray, C. (1994). *Comic strip conversations.* Arlington, TX: Future Horizons.

Vendors

Memory Scrapbooks
http://www.memoryscrapbooks.com
Get caption stickers at this site for use with written work and student-created products.

National Autism Resources
http://www.nationalautismresources.com/laminated-speech-bubbles.html
You can buy a laminated bubble here if you do not have the time to do the cutting and assembling.

Whitey Board
http://www.whiteyboard.com
All shapes and sizes of whiteboard sheets and dry erase markers are available on this site.

Web Site

Free Printables

http://www.freeprintables.org/speech-bubbles

Various printable speech bubble templates are available on this web site.

32 Handheld Directions

Materials

- Sports paddle, dowel, or wooden ruler
- Paper or cardstock
- Craft glue

Description

Many learners can "listen" better when they do not have to do so with their ears! For many students with autism, learning disabilities, and other differences, getting important directions visually helps them to "hear" the necessary information and, therefore, get the required work done or engage in expected behavior. When handheld directions are used, therefore, many learners not only are more successful, but they may be perceived as behaving better as well.

Directions

Decide on a few simple messages that you can use again and again to communicate directions or give necessary cues. For instance, you might make signs to say the following:

- Quiet, please
- Pause your conversations
- Smile
- Get ready to share one thing you just read/learned
- Line up
- Hand in papers here
- Start cleaning up
- Take a minute to check your work
- Get into base groups
- Find a partner
- Make sure you are listening to all group members
- You have 10 minutes left to work

To create your directions simply print your message on white office paper. Then, set your image on the paddle, and apply craft glue to the image and to the area around the image. Give the paddle plenty of time to dry. If you are using a dowel or ruler, write or print your message on the cardstock or cardboard and glue or otherwise fasten to the dowel or wooden ruler.

Examples

A second-grade teacher uses signs daily to "ask" students to line up, find partners, and hand in their homework.

A middle school language arts teachers uses signs to communicate silently to students as they are writing. She walks the aisles with signs that read, "Avoid trite expressions" and "Why not include a metaphor?" The signs not only give her students a smile, but provide a nonintrusive reminder about topics covered in class.

References

Kluth, P., & Kasa-Hendrickson, C. (2010). Teaching strategies. In P. Kluth (Ed.), *"You're going to love this kid!": Teaching students with autism in the inclusive classroom* (2nd ed.). Baltimore, MD: Paul H. Brookes Publishing Co.

Nelson-Sargeant, S. (2012). *Using visual cues to communicate and give directions.* Retrieved September 12, 2012, from http://www.nea.org/tools/using-visual-cues-to-communicate-and-give-directions.html

Vendors

Greek Creations
http://www.greekcreations.com/paddles/blank-paddles.aspx
Paddles of every shape and size are available on this site.

Oriental Trading
http://www.orientaltrading.com/api/search?Ntt=classroom+management
Six classroom reminder signs are available in a packet; messages include "Line up quietly" and "Raise your hand."

Web Site

Amy Laurent
http://www.amy-laurent.com
Amy Laurent offers a new visual support every month on her resource-rich web site. You can find many communication-related ideas that will help you adapt instruction and meet the needs of students with autism, learning disabilities, and cognitive disabilities.

33 "Your Turn" Sharing Stick

Materials

- Stick
- Ribbon
- Craft glue
- Other materials related to your content that students will find interesting

Description

Teachers who recognize inequities in communication time and styles in the classroom often use a talking or sharing stick to help learners monitor the number of comments they make or the amount of time they listen to others. This idea is inspired by a Native American tradition. Traditionally, these sharing sticks were used to encourage generous listening and to ensure that all points of view were heard and seen as valuable. Sharing sticks can be used during decision-making meetings, social gatherings, storytelling circles, or celebrations.

In classrooms, the practices or norms may be different, but the function of the stick is still to "give voice" to the person holding it. The stick can really be any object, but the function is always the same. It is passed from student to student during a discussion; only the person holding the stick may speak. This tool enables all students to be heard, especially those who may be shy or have communication challenges. It may also help those who are learning social skills, such as listening without talking and taking turns.

Directions

Find a stick (or better yet, ask your students to hunt for one) without many smaller branches attached. Clean it off and sand down any rough patches.

Customize the stick for your classroom. Many teachers attach (or have students attach) ribbons, fabric, or small toys/objects to represent members of the class or expected topics of discussion. An English teacher who is going to use the sharing stick to have students talk about novels and authors might attach pencil stubs or pictures of favorite authors. A music teacher might wrap her classroom stick in old sheet music or ribbons printed with musical notes.

To start using the stick in the classroom, talk to your students about why they are using a response object (e.g., to work on listening, to coax students into being more thoughtful when they speak). Also, be sure to do some modeling in the beginning. Introduce a topic, such as, "What is a goal you are setting for yourself this year?" Hold the stick in your hand and demonstrate how to be brief and respectful. Share your idea and pass the stick to a student sitting next to you. Encourage him or her to follow your example and share a reminder to be brief and respectful. Have students pass the stick around the classroom until everyone has had a chance to speak.

Examples

A middle school social studies teacher uses the sharing stick to kick off new units. Students respond to questions that ask them to connect their own personal experiences to the new content. For example, before a lesson on the American Revolution, students might answer, "What does liberty mean to you?"

A social worker in an elementary school often uses the sharing stick to get students talking about social issues at the school. She might tell them, for instance, that she has observed that some kids are not included in playground activities. Then, she may ask them to brainstorm solutions to this problem using the sharing stick.

Reference

Crowe, C. (2012). *How to bullyproof your classroom*. Turners Falls, MA: Northeast Foundation for Children.

Vendor

Native American Vault

http://www.nativeamericanvault.com

You can shop for a Native American talking stick and other Native American crafts on this site.

Web Sites

eHow

http://www.ehow.com/how_7338194_make-talking-stick.html

Tips for making your sharing stick are available on this web site.

The Responsive Classroom

http://www.responsiveclassroom.org

For more ideas about teaching listening and building your classroom community, check out this resource-rich site. The Responsive Classroom contains materials and resources that will help you increase academic achievement, decrease challenging behaviors, and create connections between learners.

34   Graffiti Table

Materials

- Classroom table
- Tape
- Butcher paper
- Markers

Description

Did you ever eat at a restaurant where they cover the tables in butcher paper and let you doodle while you wait for your meal? Usually, even the most senior members of the dinner party have fun with the gimmick and immediately start drawing, creating, tracing, and coloring.

This playful mood can be recreated in the classroom when you create graffiti tables for certain lessons or units. The idea is to allow students to take notes in an alternative fashion; instead of having them jot down their understanding of kinetic energy, let them draw examples and then compare those examples with others at their table. You also can encourage learners to draw collaboratively. This idea will thrill your doodle-loving learners.

Directions

Cut or tear a few sheets of butcher paper just large enough to cover the table. Fold the paper under the table and tape.

Section off the table if you want students to have their own areas to sketch and doodle. You could draw large squares on the paper or just lines separating the seating areas.

You can also write directions on the tables (e.g., *be sure to draw only in your designated area, draw one image every time I stop the lecture*) or add sample images along the margins of the paper. For example, if you want students to take notes on an experiment you are conducting, you could share images that students can use in graphic notetaking (e.g., change = Δ; time = $\odot$).

You can either have students draw and doodle while you are presenting a whole-class lesson (stopping at key points in the discussion to let students share their drawings), or you can let students work or read on their own and use the table to take notes at their own pace. Students can then share their drawings with others at their table at designated times.

Examples

In one arts-oriented elementary school, all first graders work on graffiti tables at least once a week. Students get to draw images based on skills that were taught during the week as part of their language arts mini-lessons. For example, they may draw rhyming words in the story this week and character traits next week.

At least once per unit, a popular biology teacher known for using many different teaching strategies, uses a version of graffiti tables. Students work four to a table during his lectures and have designated times to "stop, draw, and compare." This means that they not only have an opportunity to visually represent the learning so far, but to compare their understanding of the material with others at the table. During this time period, students often merge their drawings or make connections between images.

References

Andrade, J. (2010). What does doodling do? *Applied Cognitive Psychology, 24*(1), 100–106.

Bunyi, A. (2012). Guided reading fun with graffiti tables. Retrieved November 8, 2012, from http://www.scholastic.com/teachers/top-teaching/2012/03/guided-reading-fun-graffiti-tables

Vendors

Discount School Supply

http://www.discountschoolsupply.com

A huge selection of white and colored papers are available on this web site, including butcher paper. Their dual-surface product works especially well for this activity: one side works well for chalk, charcoal, and crayon drawing, whereas the other side works well with markers, pencils, and crayons.

Idea Paint

http://www.ideapaint.com

Turn the walls of any surface into a dry erase board using idea paint.

Web Sites

Doodler's Anonymous

http://www.doodlersanonymous.com

According to the latest research on doodling, we should not only be allowing doodling, but potentially teaching it too. This blog created for and by those who love to doodle may offer some inspiration to teachers and students in exploring a skill that should undoubtedly be more common in classrooms.

Miss Stec's Kindergarten Kollections

http://kinderkollections.blogspot.com/2012/03/graffiti-tables.html

Miss Stec, a clever kindergarten teacher, has a detailed post on her blog about using graffiti tables in guided reading. Check out her post and then stay to explore all of the fantastic lesson ideas for little ones on her site.

35 Magnetic Poetry

Materials

- Magnetic surface
- Thin magnetic sheets recycled from advertisements or purchased magnetic paper
- Labels or paper and glue

Description

Magnetic poetry is an amusing alternative to writing in any classroom. Learners who would typically balk at having to create a haiku or provide an example of hyperbole might get a real kick out of tackling those tasks with magnetic poetry.

These little magnetic words, however, also serve as a writing adaptation for students with motor problems or spelling difficulties. Instead of having to worry about the elements of production that slow them down (e.g., forming letters, considering correct spellings), students can simply focus on expressing themselves and demonstrating targeted skills.

Directions

Create your own magnetic poetry by typing out the words or phrases you want onto a label sheet (or plain paper).

If you are recycling flat magnets from retailers, peel and sand to remove the old text and images and to create a smooth and clear surface. If you are purchasing magnetic sheets instead of recycling some, you can skip this step.

Cut out the words and stick or glue them to the front of your magnets.

Finally, place them on a cookie sheet or other magnetic surface and let students create, build, and share.

Examples

A ninth-grade English teacher had students use magnetic poetry to practice several different competencies, including writing free verse, providing examples of metaphors, using alliteration, and creating "knockout" opening sentences for short stories.

A science teacher created magnetic vocabulary words to provide opportunities for students to play with new terminology (literally). The magnets also served as a support for a student who struggled with writing tasks.

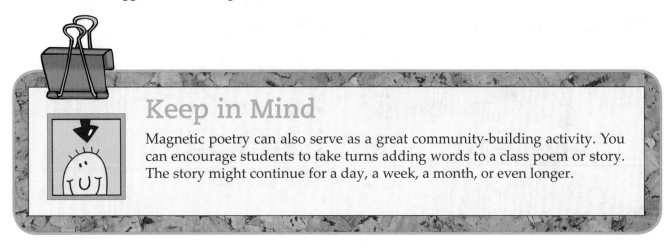

Keep in Mind

Magnetic poetry can also serve as a great community-building activity. You can encourage students to take turns adding words to a class poem or story. The story might continue for a day, a week, a month, or even longer.

Reference

Berkey, S. (2009). *Teaching the moving child: OT insights that will transform your K-3 classroom.* Baltimore, MD: Paul H. Brookes Publishing Co.

Vendors

Avery

http://www.avery.com

Avery offers various sizes of labels for sale.

Magnetic Poetry

http://www.magneticpoetry.com

This company was the first to create, sell, and market those little kits many of us have purchased for refrigerators, dorm rooms, and classrooms. Their recently updated site features many products you can buy, as well as free games for kids. Check the kids' area to drag and drop virtual magnets and write poetry with a tap of the finger.

Web Site

Giggle Poetry

http://www.gigglepoetry.com

Meadowbrook Press has an entire web site dedicated to humorous poetry for children. Check it out to give students ideas for their own creations.

36 Dialogue Journals

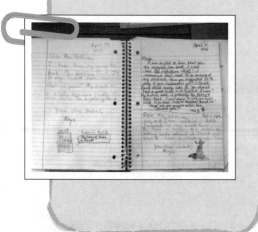

Materials

- Notebook
- Different colors of pens/pencils
- Stickers or stamps

Description

A dialogue journal is a written conversation in which a student and teacher communicate regularly over a semester, school year, or course. Students write as much as they choose and the teacher writes back, responding to students' comments, introducing new topics, or asking questions. The teacher is a participant in an ongoing, written conversation with the student, rather than an evaluator who corrects or comments on the student's writing.

Directions

Give each one of your students a personal notebook to use as their dialogue journal. To start the process, you may give a prompt, such as, "What is one thing I don't know about you but should?"

After the first one or two "conversations," you will not need a prompt because the conversation you are having with the learner will provide plenty of opportunities for discussion.

You can ask students questions, prompt them to comment on a quote or thought, or even add trivia questions, jokes, or puzzles.

Typically, dialogue journals are not formally assessed. Most teachers, however, do read them to get information about student growth and add comments and questions that will help the progress of individual students.

Examples

A co-teaching team in the high school set up a dialogue notebook for a 10th-grade student with Down syndrome. The journal was used as a way to create a social opportunity for the young man with a disability, but it also served as a literacy support.

Teachers in one elementary school were encouraged to set up dialogue journals with individual learners who either needed more writing support or required enrichment as writers. The journals allowed teachers to regularly assess the writing of individual students and gather information about the most effective next steps in writing instruction.

Keep in Mind

The teacher is not the only possible partner for a dialogue journal. Anyone in the building can serve as a journal partner. A literacy coach, occupational therapist, speech and language pathologist, paraprofessional, older student/tutor, or administrator can also be a student's partner.

References

Bailes, C. (1999). Dialogue journals: Fellowship, conversation, and English modeling. *Perspectives in Education and Deafness, 17*(5), 10–13.

Ewald, J.D. (2004). Students' evaluations of dialogue journals: Perspectives on classroom themes. *Applied Language Learning, 14,* 37–53.

Peyton, J.K., & Staton, J. (1993). *Dialogue journals in the multilingual classroom: Building language fluency and writing skills through written interaction.* Norwood, NJ: Ablex.

Schleper, D.R. (2000). Dialogue journals … for students, teachers, and parents. *Odyssey, 1*(2), 11–14.

Vendor

Bare Books

http://www.barebooks.com

If you want students to use something other than a spiral notebook, you could let them create a customized journal complete with a student-created cover.

Web Sites

Journaling Arts

http://journalingarts.wordpress.com/

Dialogue notebooks are just the beginning of what is possible when you get a little creative with the practice of journaling. This is one of many blogs on the web that explores materials, formats, and the purposes of writing.

You Can Teach Writing

http://blog.you-can-teach-writing.com

Linda Aragoni's ideas will be helpful to any writing teacher but especially to those teaching young adults and adults.

Two Writing Teachers

http://twowritingteachers.wordpress.com

If you want more resources on teaching writing, you will want to bookmark this site. On Two Writing Teachers, you will find lesson plan ideas, great literature related to writing, and many reflections on teaching.

37 Reading Phones

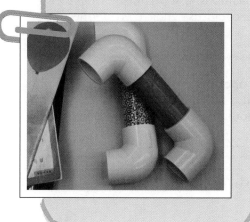

Materials

- PVC pipe (2.75-inch elbow joints and 0.75-inch PVC pipe cut into a 4.5-inch piece)
- PVC glue
- Duct tape

Description

If you have students with auditory sensitivity in your classroom, you will want to introduce reading phones to help cut out background noise and promote reading fluency. Many learners on the autism spectrum, for example, struggle to stay focused in a busy classroom. They may notice children screaming at the playground or the chatting voices of classmates. Reading phones can help students focus on their own voice during a reading lesson while cutting out any interfering noise in the environment.

The phone can also help students learn to use a softer voice when independently reading or partner reading in the classroom. Because the student's voice is amplified when they use their phone, the student learns quickly to use a softer voice.

Reading phones also tend to be a fun addition to the classroom. Bringing in an item that is not only seen as unique but even a bit silly can result in less classroom boredom and more interested readers.

Directions

Take your PVC pipe segment and apply PVC glue to both ends of the segment.
Attach the elbow joints.
Set your phones down on newspaper or other covered surface and let dry.
Attach ribbons or duct tape to the phones to personalize them for your students or let students decorate to match their moods, personalities, or interests.

Examples

A kindergarten teacher offered reading phones to her English language learners during her literacy centers, but found that many other students requested to use them. She then created enough for all students in the classroom so that anyone could use their own phone during literacy activities.

An elementary school music teacher offered a reading phone to one of her students with Asperger syndrome during certain lessons. She found that it helped him focus on written materials. The student even did better performing when he could occasionally listen to his singing voice through the phone.

A high school French teacher used reading phones at one of her learning stations to have students practice their pronunciation of new words.

Reference

Hudson, R.F., Lane, H.B., & Pullen, P.C. (2005). Reading fluency assessment and instruction: What, why, and how? *The Reading Teacher, 58,* 702–714.

Vendor

Whisper Phone

http://www.whisperphone.com

You can shop for phones here, learn about relevant research, and get ideas for phone-related lessons.

Web Site

LD Online

http://www.ldonline.org

If you like this idea and want more information on supporting students with reading disabilities and related challenges, check out LD Online.

38 Quick Quip Keychains

Materials

- Keychain ring
- Keychains with message windows

Description

To encourage participation in daily lessons, some of your students may benefit from quick and easy supplements to their primary communication systems. Quick quip keychains are not enough to meet all or even most of a student's communication needs, but they can work well in environments where students do not have easy access to their other systems (e.g., school bus) or in situations where just a few messages will do the trick.

Directions

Evaluate a student's environments and activities to find "holes" where the learner may benefit from increased access to communication. Then, decide which messages might be needed for that particular situation or activity. If the student cannot brainstorm with you, turn to peers for ideas or listen to learners as they interact in that situation or during that activity. Make your decisions based on these auditory observations.

Once you have an idea about the phrases that should be included, write or type the messages or prompts on small slips of paper and pop them into your keychain's message window. Clip your keychain in a spot convenient for the user. It could go on a student's house keys, their binder, their backpack, or even on their wheelchair or walker.

Examples

A high school student carries a quick quip keychain with him on his house key ring. He can access simple messages such as "Hello," "How are you?" and "Do you want to see my photos?" This last statement is related to his interest in taking pictures of buildings and churches with his cell phone. He loves to both take photos daily and share them with interested classmates.

A second-grade student uses his quick quip keychain during reading buddies lessons. He and his partner indicate when they think something is funny, when they want to read something again, or when they really like or dislike a book.

Reference

Spears, C.L, Turner, V., & Diaz, P. (2011). *Rising to new heights of communication and learning for children with autism: The definitive guide to using alternative-augmentative communication, visual strategies, and learning supports at home and school.* London, UK: Jessica Kingsley.

Vendors

I Need Help Communication Bracelets
http://www.ineedhelpcommunicationbracelets.com

These bracelets help individuals with communication differences identify emotions, needs, wants, and preferences.

Qcharm
http://www.qcharm.com

Qcharm is a portable visual viewing system. These picture bracelets can serve as daily schedules, visual prompts, or communication supports.

Web Site

International Society for Augmentative and Alternative Communication
https://www.isaac-online.org/english/home

The International Society for Augmentative and Alternative Communication (ISAAC) works to improve the lives of children and adults who use AAC. ISAAC's vision is that AAC will be recognized, valued, and used throughout the world.

39 Communication Kits

Materials

- AlphaSmart or electronic tablet
- Sign language cards
- Book of common communication symbols
- Dry erase board and markers
- Cookbook holder/slant board
- Talking photo album
- Single-message communicators
- Recordable books, greeting cards, and keychains
- Hook and loop tape
- Label maker

Description

Sometimes it is hard to assess exactly what types of communication supports a student will need for a particular task. In these instances, it can be helpful to have a richly stocked communication kit in the classroom that can be accessed by students with disabilities. These materials are often of interest to students without disabilities as well, so it can be helpful to find ways for all students to occasionally use the AAC tools in the kit. This practice may increase the likelihood that students with or without disabilities will help to generate adaptation ideas during lessons and across classroom activities. Materials will vary depending on the needs of your students.

Directions

Work with your school's speech pathologist to stock your kit. In addition, search the Internet for downloadable picture symbols and visual supports to create. Finally, search the classroom for low-tech augmentative communication options, such as sign language flashcards, recordable books and greeting cards, a dry erase board, and homemade pointers.

Example

A second-grade teacher created a kit for use during learning centers. Students could dialogue with a partner on paper, create a poem using only the sign language vocabulary cards found in the kit, or design their own content-related communication boards. The communication kit was always available at this station to support students in their learning.

References

Beukelman, D., & Mirenda, P. (2013). *Augmentative and alternative communication: Supporting children and adults with complex communication needs* (4th ed.). Baltimore, MD: Paul H. Brookes Publishing Co.

Mirenda, P., & Iacono, T. (2009). *Autism spectrum disorders and AAC.* Baltimore, MD: Paul H. Brookes Publishing Co.

Soto, G., & Zangari, C. (Eds.). (2009). *Practically speaking: Language, literacy, and academic development for students with AAC needs.* Baltimore, MD: Paul H. Brookes Publishing Co.

Vendors

DynaVox

http://www.dynavoxtech.com

DynaVox is a developer, manufacturer, and distributor of speech-generating devices. They also carry a variety of related accessories.

Enablemart

http://www.enablemart.com

EnableMart has hundreds of devices from many different manufacturers.

Web Site

The Assistive Technology Blog

http://www.assistivetechnology.vcu.edu

Published by the Virginia Department of Education's Training and Technical Assistance Center, this blog is one of the very best for finding low-tech and high-tech solutions for the classroom. It features short, informative posts about assistive technology and AAC.

40 Rotating Reader

Materials

- Rolodex
- Rolodex cards
- Markers
- Magazines
- Stickers

Description

If you have students with difficulty turning pages, consider placing content on the pages of a rotating file device, such as a Rolodex. Not only does this idea qualify as ecofriendly because you will most likely be recycling a piece of office equipment your school or district is no longer using, but it is an elegant and simple adaptation that many learners find both appealing and easy to use.

Directions

You can create your rotating reader for students or with them. The first step is to identify the content you wish to share on the reader. Consider content that all students or your target student need to access. This may include vocabulary words and definitions for standardized tests, writing prompts, favorite snippets of dialogue, short poems, or examples of figurative language. Keep in mind you will have to choose material that will easily fit on the Rolodex cards.

Then, introduce the reader to your student or students. Demonstrate how you want the student to use the reader (e.g., to review for an upcoming quiz, to find and share content with classmates).

Finally, provide some class time for the learner to use the reader. If a student is using the reader to collect and review story problems, for instance, you may want to give him 5 minutes each week to lead a class mini lesson.

Examples

A middle school teacher created a rotating poetry reader for her classroom. Originally it was created for a student on the autism spectrum who loved the television show *The Office*. The teacher knew that the young man would be delighted to have his poems mounted on the Rolodex cards because he was thrilled any time he got to use office supplies like his favorite character, Michael Scott. Eventually, however, all of the students became interested in the rotating reader. Other students used it to find poems to share for a "reading of the day" classroom ritual. Many learners also added original poetry to the reader.

A rotating reader was created for a third-grade student with significant motor planning problems. Jokes, riddles, inspirational quotes, and fun facts were added both by the teacher and by other students. Students used it in morning meeting and during their periodic "open mic" Fridays where students took turns sharing in front of the class.

References

Erickson, K. & Koppenhaver, D. (2007). *Children with disabilities: Reading and writing the four-blocks way.* Greensboro, NC: Carson-Dellosa.

Kasa-Hendrickson, C., & Kluth, P. (2005). "We have to start with inclusion and work it out as we go": Successful inclusion for non-verbal students with autism. *Journal of Whole Schooling, 2,* 2–14.

Kluth, P., & Chandler-Olcott, K. (2007). *A land we can share: Teaching literacy to students with autism.* Baltimore, MD: Paul H. Brookes Publishing Co.

Vendors

Inside Story Flashcards

http://insidestoryflashcards.com

If you do not have time to create your own content, you can fill your rotating reader with fun flashcards like the unique and captivating vocabulary cards available on this site.

Office Depot

http://www.officedepot.com

Despite the fact that many people have switched to storing contact information electronically, there is still a market for rotating file systems. Office Depot and several other large chains still carry the Rolodex brand.

Web Site

Glenda's Assistive Technology Information and More...

http://atclassroom.blogspot.com

Glenda is not only up on all of the newer high-tech ideas (e.g., apps and tablets), but she keeps us informed about the best in low-tech too with great posts on visual schedules, page fluffing, and the use of keyguards for student devices.

Behavior & Motivation

Contents

41   Goal-Setting Cards 98

42   Check-In Tents 100

43   Timers 102

44   Purposeful Puzzles 105

45   Mantra Reminders 107

46   Classifieds 109

47   Special Interest Swag 111

48   Break Slips 113

49   Scratch-Off Lottery Cards 115

50   Social Skill Slam Book 117

41 Goal-Setting Cards

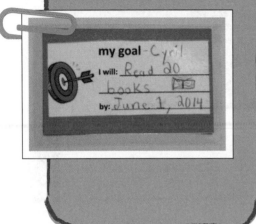

Materials

- Blank business cards
- Markers or colored pencils
- Stickers
- Laminating machine

Description

As teachers, we spend a lot of time setting goals for students. However, how much time do we spend letting students set some of their own goals? How many books do students want to read? What grades do they want? What after-school activities do they want to pursue? What score do they want on the test? What skills do they want to acquire? All of these questions are appropriate for students to answer, potentially set goals around, and record on goal-setting cards.

Not only can goal setting be very motivating for young people, but it can provide them with a life skill that can be applied to their personal and work lives down the road. Further it allows students to do some differentiating on their own. Their goals are their own and will likely be completely different from those created by any other learner in the class.

Directions

Start by sharing some of your own goals. Be sure to provide examples that are measurable and observable; in other words, it should be clear to everyone what the goal or desired behavior is (that is the observable part) and what must happen for the goal to be achieved. A goal of *becoming a more serious student* is not measurable and observable, but a goal of *getting a B on every test until the end of the year* is both observable and measurable. Anyone wanting to assess the student's success on this goal would know what to look for and would know whether or not the goal had been met.

You might decide to create general goal cards with students or to target certain subject areas or activities. Once the cards are created, ask student volunteers to share their goals. Then, have students talk to one another about their plans for implementation. Ask them to consider how they plan to address their goals, how they are going to deal with obstacles, and how they are going to assess their progress.

Ask students for progress reports on their goals on a regular basis. Throughout the year, offer success stories on goal setting and share strategies for meeting personal goals.

Examples

Sixth-grade students set goals for themselves for the school year and for their middle school career. Students set both academic and school-related goals (e.g., read 20 books per year, play *The Orange Blossom Special* on violin, run a 5-km race) and personal goals (e.g., talk to my grandmother every week, learn to play chess, eat a healthy breakfast every day).

Students at one high school are asked to attend their own individualized education program (IEP) meetings and cofacilitate them, if possible. Students not only give their own reports about progress, but they come with their own ideas for goals. Learners are then encouraged to make cards for any goal that is particularly important to them.

References

Brown, D. (2008). *Goal setting for children with learning disabilities: Your role is important.* Retrieved April 10, 2013, from http://www.ldonline.org/article/21026

Schunk, D.H. (2003). Self-efficacy for reading and writing: Influence of modeling, goal setting, and self-evaluation. *Reading and Writing Quarterly, 19,* 159–172.

Shteynberg, G., & Galinsky, A.D. (2011). Implicit coordination: Sharing goals with similar others intensifies goal pursuit. *Journal of Experimental Social Psychology, 47,* 1291–1294.

Vendor

KidsDiscuss.com

http://www.kidsdiscuss.com/parent_resource_center.asp?pr_id=kd004

Jean Tracy created a goal-setting kit for kids that is available on this web site.

Web Site

Larry Ferlazzo

http://larryferlazzo.edublogs.org/2010/05/18/my-best-posts-on-students-setting-goals

Larry Ferlazzo updates his blog daily and writes about a variety of topics, including English language learners, technology, school–home connections, and student motivation. He posts frequently about goal setting and student empowerment. This link brings you to some of his best posts on goals.

42 Check-In Tents

Materials

- Tag board
- Paper
- Glue
- Packing tape or laminate

Description

One of the challenges of facilitating a busy classroom is assessing how students are doing as they progress through tasks independently. This is especially difficult in a differentiated classroom where all learners may not be working on the same tasks or using the same materials. To make this task easier, some educators rely on check-in tents. These simple visual supports not only make it easier for teachers to know how the entire class is doing at a glance and provide support to those students who need it, but they also help learners pay attention to their level of comprehension, independence, and ability when working on their own.

Directions

Fold tag board into thirds. Create messages on a document adding any graphics necessary for non-readers. Print, cut, and paste one message to each of the three sections. Laminate or "seal" with packing tape.

Provide instruction on how and when you want students to use their tents. Some teachers like them on desks only during certain activities, whereas others may use them during all seat work, independent work, and small-group tasks.

Example

Second- and third-grade students in a multiage classroom used their tents during all independent and small-group math activities. The three sides of their tents read, *I have a question, I'm finished,* and *I am working.* Students with *I am finished* signs may be approached to help other students, move to new activities, or work with the teacher.

Reference

Tomlinson, C.A., & Imbeau, M.B. (2010). *Leading and managing a differentiated classroom.*
   Alexandria, VA: ASCD.

Vendor

Staples
http://www.staples.com/Tent-Cards/cat_CL141307
Staples offers tent cards that you may use for this project.

Web Site

Time 4 Organization
http://time4organization.blogspot.com
This blog provides lots of student support and organization ideas.

43 Timers

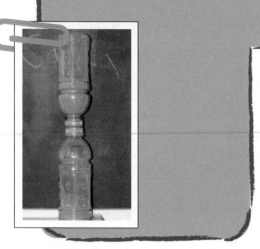

Materials

- Sand
- Drink bottles of equal size
- Clean sand
- Tornado tube
- Marker

Description

Timers can be put to good use in maintaining pace in lessons, helping students keep focused, and encouraging time management. They are also helpful for students who may need the comfort of knowing "how long" they are required to stay with an activity, especially those that may be challenging or unfamiliar to the individual.

Directions

Peel the labels off the bottles. Wash them out and let them dry completely.

Fill one of the bottles half full of sand. Screw the tornado tube into the top of this bottle, then screw the other bottle into the free end of the tornado tube. Alternatively, you can drill small holes in two bottle caps and tape your bottles together.

Turn the bottles over so the bottle with sand in it is now on top. The sand will flow down into the bottom bottle. Use the stopwatch to time how long it takes.

Upend your sand timer again and time how long it takes all the sand to go through once more. As the sand falls, mark the sand level in the top bottle at regular intervals. For example, you could mark where the sand level is every 10 or 15 seconds. Keep marking until all the sand has run out. Now you can use your timer to actually tell how much time has passed by counting interval marks.

Once students have their timers, they can be used for many different purposes, including the actual teaching of time (e.g., "How long is 10 minutes?"), waiting or taking turns, breaking challenging times of the day into manageable intervals, implementing a deep breathing or relaxation time before assessments, inspiring good habits (e.g., cleaning up at the end of the day, reading for 10 minutes when you finish other work), and implementing time guidelines into class meetings or group discussions. Timers can even be used in the context of certain lessons such as those on gravity, measurement, or rate.

Examples

Students in a fourth-grade classroom made their own sand timers, put their names on them, and stored them in a materials closet. They were asked to pull them out and use them for certain activities, such as timed tests. The students could also choose to use them for other activities, such as managing their time during project-based instruction.

A science teacher had all of her students create their own timers during a science lab. The students created 3-minute, 5-minute, and 10-minute timers for their classroom. The teacher then used the new timers during math drills and for breaks in the classroom.

Co-teachers in a fifth-grade classroom used their 60-second timer for fluency drills or to teach new vocabulary words. Students worked in pairs at a center, setting the timer and then reading and defining as many of the vocabulary words as they could in 60 seconds.

A student with Asperger syndrome used her homemade timers throughout the school day to visually assess the time available for certain tasks. She was also called upon by the teacher to be the timekeeper for several class activities such as class jobs, mental math problems, and cram sessions before tests.

Reference

Iovannone, R., Dunlap, G., Huber, H., & Kincaid, D. (2003). Effective educational practices for students with autism spectrum disorders. *Focus on Autism and Other Developmental Disabilities, 18*(3), 150–165.

Vendors

Time Timer
http://www.timetimer.com
Search this site to find timers, accessories, and tips for using timers in the classroom.

Fiery Ideas
http://www.fieryideas.com/the-supertimer-19-c.asp
The Fiery Ideas site has a free Super Timer with goofy graphics and a related audio track that may be appealing to some.

Web Sites

Teachit Timer

http://www.teachit.co.uk/custom_content/timer/clock3.html

This useful flash-based timer allows you to keep time, from seconds up to hours. You can choose to display the timer, the clock version, or both. You also can select from a series of alarms to mark the point at which the timer reaches zero.

Class Tools

http://www.classtools.net

This site provides a countdown timer that can be paired with a selection of different sound-tracks, including Mozart, *Star Wars*, and *Hawaii 5-0*.

44 Purposeful Puzzles

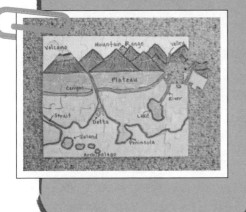

Materials

- Blank puzzle
- Colored pencils or markers

Description

Purposeful puzzles are so named because they are a first and foremost a fun activity, but they can also be put into classrooms to serve a specific purpose or teach a particular piece of content.

Puzzles are an especially helpful support for students who might fidget a lot during class or need to be "doing something" when they are listening or participating in a classroom discussion. Some students doodle to meet this need, but others may appreciate a support that directly helps them learn targeted content.

Directions

To get ideas for puzzles, look at content-area standards for information and ideas that students need to know and understand. You might also scan textbooks for important charts, diagrams, maps, descriptions, and images. Once you have found a puzzle idea, sketch your drawing lightly with a pencil on the blank puzzle page so that any errors can be changed easily. Then, color with markers or colored pencils to make the image easy to assemble. Be sure to add any important vocabulary words and facts.

Provide students with directions for how and when to use their puzzles. Encourage learners to share their finished products with classmates.

Example

A student with Down syndrome was sometimes fidgety during his social studies class. A teaching assistant on the middle school team created a series of standards-based puzzles that could double as desktop fidgets, be used as repeating homework assignments, and serve as study guides for the most important ideas in a unit. The content on the puzzles was always complex, so any learner could use them to study and learn.

Reference

McDonald, E.S., & Hershman, D.M. (2010). *Classrooms that spark: Recharge and revive your teaching.* San Francisco, CA: Jossey Bass.

Vendors

Puzzle Warehouse

http://www.puzzlewarehouse.com

You can order a 36-piece blank floor puzzle here, as well as a 99-piece tabletop jigsaw puzzle.

Puzzles for Sale

http://www.puzzlesforsale.com

Explore this site to find puzzles for all ages, of many different sizes, and for many different subject areas, including birds, folk art, the *Titanic,* and cities of the world.

Yoyo.com

http://www.yoyo.com

This web site offers 63-piece blank puzzles.

Web Site

Jigsaw Puzzles

http://www.neok12.com/jigsaw-puzzles.htm

This web site provides virtual jigsaw puzzles with many themes including the human eye, lasers, the French Revolution, and natural disasters.

45　Mantra Reminders

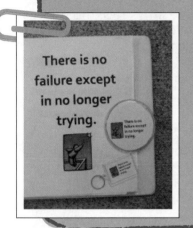

Materials

- Business cards
- Paper
- Magnets
- Page protectors
- Key chains

Description

Mantras are short, powerful, positive messages that students can use to shift their thoughts and hopefully change their behavior. The goal of using mantras in the classroom is to help students internalize positive ways of thinking, encourage helpful and productive self-talk, and introduce a process that can be used not only in the present, but in any future situation or environment. In other words, great mantras or slogans (e.g., "There is no failure except failing to try") may not only help a student get through homework challenges, but they also may carry him or her through the spelling bee, cheerleading tryouts, and job interviews.

Directions

First, talk to students about slogans, affirmations, and mantras in your own life. Have learners discuss any mantras they already use in school, their personal lives, sports, and so on. Then have students select a few mantras that they might adopt for their own use. Share a list of examples, if necessary.

After the students have found some mantras that might work in their own lives, create pocket-sized reminders by printing them on business cards and tucking them in the students' desks, wallets, lockers, or binders.

Mantra reminders can be created in all sizes and formats. We have placed pages inside students' notebooks, put magnets inside their lockers, created key chains to hang on for their backpacks, and even printed inspiring slogans on their shirts.

Example

Several mantra products were created for a high school student with learning disabilities who struggled with making errors. He was a perfectionist who reacted negatively to any perceived failure, including imperfect test scores and not placing first in cross-country races. This student adopted two mantras: *errors are opportunities* and *let it go … and learn*. He made stickers of his slogans and posted them on his sporting equipment and in his locker.

Reference

D'Alessio, R. (2011). *Bringing our souls to the classroom.* Bloomington, IN: Balboa.

Vendor

BSL Creations

http://bslcreations.com

Several different mantra-related products are available on this site. The Kids Inspirational Card Deck, for example, contains these messages: *I am happy to be me, I know some kids won't like me and that is okay,* and *I can be angry without hurting people or things.*

Web Sites

Abundance Tapestry

http://www.abundancetapestry.com/101-affirmations-for-children

This web site offers 101 positive mantras to teach to young people.

The Affirmation Spot

http://theaffirmationspot.wordpress.com/2012/01/30/student-and-learning-affirmations

Dozens of affirmations for the classroom are available.

46 Classifieds

Materials

- Bulletin board
- Paper

Description

Students in diverse, inclusive classrooms are certainly resources for one another, but educators may not quite know how to communicate this message in a concrete way. Some teachers choose to share this information in the context of class meetings. Others may create class directories. A few may choose to be even more clear and explicit by designing an advertisement board in the classroom to showcase one "help wanted" and one classified section offering from each learner. Students might ask for help with math tests and offer support in learning to knit, playing piano, or mastering a new technology.

Directions

Distribute small pieces of paper to each student with instructions to create two advertisements. One advertisement should offer a service or support to someone, whereas the other should ask for assistance with a specific task. Attach the advertisements in a place where students can easily view them.

Then, give students time to formally browse the boards and take notes on the offerings and needs. Once students have a sense of what is posted, build in regular opportunities for "ad answering." That is, give students time to either work together to support one another or—at the very least—give them time to set appointments with one another for collaboration. You may not be able to use class time to have students teach each other karate, but you can let them schedule in recess time with each other to address this goal.

Example

An entire fifth-grade class put up classified advertisements to showcase their needs and strengths. Throughout the year, students were given strategies to access the skills and gifts of their classmates. An option during some indoor recess periods and some lunch periods was to get a lesson from someone on the board. For example, students could ask for a calligraphy lesson or be given help organizing their desks.

Reference

Sapon-Shevin, M. (2010). *Because we can change the world: A practical guide to building cooperative, inclusive classroom communities.* Thousand Oaks, CA: Corwin.

Vendor

Carson-Dellosa Publishing
http://www.carsondellosa.com/cd2/searchcatalog.aspx?k=productTypeGroup:Bulletin+Board+Sets
Bulletin board sets of all colors and themes are available on this web site.

Web Site

Mara Sapon-Shevin
http://www.marasapon-shevin.org
For even more community-building ideas, visit the web site of Mara Sapon-Shevin, which is filled with resources related to inclusive schooling.

47 Special Interest Swag

Materials

- Small box or container
- Items related to a student's special interests

Description

School can be a very stressful place for students on the autism spectrum or for those with anxiety disorders. These students may spend their days worried and tense. One way teachers can help is to tap into the special interests of their students and offer time with preferred materials. Many students who are able to spend some time with favorite items can better regulate their emotions and even remain calmer in crisis.

Directions

Once you have identified the student's special interests, find objects to represent these interests and place them in a small container in or near the student's desk. The student can also be asked to bring or suggest objects for the collection. Typical items include photographs, small tokens, good-luck charms, newspaper clippings, small stuffed toys, ornaments, figurines, fidgets, and laminated quotes, cartoons, or notes. The items can all represent the same theme or the student might identify different items for specific worries. Preferences might change throughout the school year, so check in with the student to see if their "swag" needs to be updated from time to time.

The guidelines for using the box can be negotiated as they will undoubtedly change throughout the year. Individual students will also need different guidelines as supports will vary depending on levels of need, age, and other factors.

Examples

A second-grade teacher knew that a student in her class loved turtles, so she helped the student fill the box with a turtle eraser top, a picture of the student with his pet turtle, and a card with a picture of a cartoon turtle yelling, "Go away worries!"

A preschool teacher used a large container to create a calm-down area in the classroom. Several of her students used the space and the "swag" as tools for regulation and relaxation. The container included favorite stuffed animals, toy trains, and an empty case from a favorite transportation-themed video.

A high school teacher used an e-tablet, a drawing pad, and a 1,000-piece puzzle station as calming items. During advisory or after a stressful assignment, a student with anxiety issues was allowed to isolate himself within the classroom and use one of the items to relax.

References

Kluth, P., & Schwarz, P. (2008). *Just give him the whale! 20 ways to use fascinations, areas of expertise, and strengths to support students with autism.* Baltimore, MD: Paul H. Brookes Publishing Co.

Kluth, P., & Schwarz, P. (2010). *Pedro's whale.* Baltimore, MD: Paul H. Brookes Publishing Co.

Winter-Messiers, M.A. (2007). From tarantulas to toilet brushes: Understanding the special interest areas of children and youth with Asperger syndrome. *Remedial and Special Education, (28)*3, 140–152.

Vendor

Oriental Trading

http://www.orientaltrading.com

You can shop for pocket-sized toys and trinkets here.

Web Sites

Patrick Schwarz

http://www.patrickschwarz.com

Dr. Patrick Schwarz has authored two books on using fascinations in the classroom. His web site is a resource for those interested in this topic or inclusive schooling in general.

Paula Kluth

http://www.paulakluth.com/readings/autism/thank-you-bob-barker

Paula has an article on her web site about teaching with fascinations and writes regularly about using special interests in the classroom.

48 Break Slips

Materials

- Index cards
- Laminator
- Hook and loop tape

Description

All of us need to take breaks throughout the day, and our students are no different. A student may ask to use the restroom or get a drink of water as a way to take a break from work or an overstimulating environment. A common accommodation seen on many education plans is to allow these breaks, and a common goal on plans is to teach students to request them.

Directions

Cut a piece of card stock, construction paper, or an index card into a small rectangle that can easily fit into the student's pocket. Write the words *I need a break* on the card and laminate each card. You can change the verbiage for older students to *Taking 5* or some other message chosen by the learner.

Decide on the number of breaks that the student will need during the school day by using some baseline data. Usually breaks are given after challenging tasks have been completed or when the classroom or school day has been very busy. At the beginning of the school day, give the student the break cards that are allowed for the day and let the student decide when to use them. By providing them with the cards at the beginning of the day, it makes it clear to the student how many breaks will be allowed but also provides the freedom to use them over a long period of time.

What constitutes a break will depend on the needs of each student. Talking walks, spending time alone, helping out in the library, reading, or playing learning games on the computer are possible options.

Breaks are a preventative strategy so you will want to give your students who use them time away from demands throughout the day even if they are calm or successfully participating. In other words, do not wait until your students get agitated before offering a break.

Example

A middle school student with mental health challenges was dealing with depression. The student used breaks as a way to regroup throughout his school day. He had 10 break cards to use each week.

Keep in Mind

If you are introducing breaks for the first time to a younger student, you might want to display the cards on his or her desktop. This way the student has a clear visual of how many breaks are left at any given time. This strategy can be used to teach self-monitoring. Older students don't have one desk so they can keep the cards in their pockets and hand them to the teacher discreetly and without any explanation. As students get older, they often worry about standing out. By using break cards they can assess their own needs, work independently, and take steps to create the most comfortable learning experience possible for themselves.

Reference

Endow, J. (2009). *Outsmarting explosive behavior: A visual system of support and intervention for individuals with autism spectrum disorders.* Shawnee Mission, KS: Autism Asperger Publishing.

Vendor

MPM School Supplies
http://www.mpmschoolsupplies.com/c-277-hall-passes-door-hangers.aspx
A variety of hall passes that can serve as discrete indicators of the need for a break.

Web Site

Hands in Autism
http://www.handsinautism.org/tools.html
Templates are available for break cards and other visual supports.

49 Scratch-Off Lottery Cards

Materials

- Cardstock
- Contact paper
- Silver metallic acrylic paint
- Liquid dish soap

Description

Everyone wants to win the lottery, so bring that wishful spirit into the classroom by creating your own scratch-off cards. The cards can be used as a tool for engaging learners and differentiating instruction. Scratch-offs can be used as a novelty item in stations or centers, as a funny alternative homework assignment, as a quirky gift to students, or as a tool for honoring the interests of individual students.

Directions

Use the cardstock as the lottery card and draw or write answers, rewards, riddles, or mystery homework assignments right on the card. "Laminate" the cards with contact paper to make them reusable. Mix two parts of the metallic acrylic paint and one part of liquid soap to create the scratch-off material. Paint over your words or images completely.

Have students use a coin or sharp object to scratch off their tickets.

Examples

One Monday a month, a fifth-grade teacher used scratch-off tickets to assign homework. Instead of their typical assignments, students picked scratch-off cards to get their assignments. They might be assigned to read a comic book, do a good deed, research a bizarre world record, make a 1-minute movie, or write a postcard. Even though students thought the assignments were random, the clever teacher used the lottery cards as an opportunity to differentiate homework assignments. A student learning English, for instance, was almost always given homework that involved communication, vocabulary, and learning about the community. For instance, his scratch-off card once directed him to conduct a 5-minute interview with a neighbor.

Students in one middle school classroom were rewarded with scratch-off tickets when they contributed to the classroom community in some way (e.g., helped someone with classwork, donated a book to the classroom library). All of the scratch-off cards featured corny jokes. Students had to scratch their cards to get to the punch line. A student with disabilities loved to get the scratch-off tickets, and he kept them to share with friends and family. The teachers therefore crafted jokes for him that contained words he could read or those they wanted him to learn.

A high school teacher had some English language learners and also students with lower reading levels, so she occasionally used the scratch-off cards as a vocabulary game at one of the learning stations in her English class. Learners would see their vocabulary word on the card and then four options for a synonym. The student had to make the correct choice to win a prize listed at the bottom.

Reference

Otten, K., & Tuttle, J. (2011). *How to reach and teach children with challenging behavior: Practical, ready-to-use interventions that work.* San Francisco, CA: Jossey Bass.

Vendors

Easy Scratch Offs

http://www.easyscratchoffs.com

If you do not want to paint your own cards, you can buy these scratch-off stickers and simply place them over the words and images on your cards.

Really Good Stuff

http://search.reallygoodstuff.com

You will find many useful tools for creating a motivating classroom on this teacher supply web site. Be sure to check out their incentive tickets and their classroom ticket organizer, in particular.

Web Sites

A Teacher's Treasure

http://www.ateacherstreasure.com/2011/07/incentives-pinterest-project-3.html

Mrs. Zrihen, creator of A Teacher's Treasure, uses her blog as an outlet for sharing "tidbids and treasures" from her classroom. She regularly features teacher-created materials that educators can use to motivate and support learners. Read including this post on how she used lottery tickets in her classroom.

Tonya's Treats for Teachers

http://tonyastreatsforteachers.blogspot.com/2012/06/monday-made-it-turned-into-give-way.html

Tonya, a third-grade teacher, shares the classroom lottery tickets she made on her blog. She shows a couple of themes and gives ideas for prizes that can be revealed to learners.

50 Social Skill Slam Book

Materials

- Notebook or binder
- Photographs of students
- Speech bubble stickers

Description

Did you have a slam book as a kid? We remember using slam books to share favorite things, classroom crushes, and recommendations for friends. If you are not familiar with slam books, the concept is simple. The owner of the book creates a roster on the front cover or first page of the book with a series of numbers and one name next to each one. Then, on each subsequent page of the book, a question is posted along with a numbered list. Students answer each question by providing their response next to the number they are assigned at the beginning of the book. So, a student who signed in as the seventh name on the first page answers every subsequent question on line 7. Since names only show up on the first page, some slam book owners tear out that information so the content is private to anyone else viewing the book. This allows contributors to freely share information such as "What was your most embarrassing moment?" Questions for typical slam books range from *What is your favorite ice cream?* to *Who do you have a crush on?* to *Who is a person you admire?*

This idea is a slight variation of the slam books we grew up using. Our slam books are not necessarily as exciting as those found in the back of the classroom, but they feature that spirit of togetherness and secret-sharing just the same.

Directions

Teachers can create social skill slam books for their students who need advice and guidance from peers on topics such as making friends and dealing with stress. To help visual learners, this format includes pictures of classmates instead of just their words of advice.

First, decide on the social skills you want to target and develop simple questions based on these skills. Sample questions include the following:

- What are some topics you like to discuss with your friends?
- How do you know your conversation partner wants to change the topic?

- How do you start a conversation with someone new?
- How do you deal with anxiety?
- How do you deal with perfectionism?
- What do you do to calm down when you are really upset?
- How do you handle unfair situations?
- How do you cope with a low grade?
- How do you find the right extracurricular activity?

Then, ask your student with social challenges to choose a few peers he or she respects and would like to use as advisors.

On the first page of your book, introduce the advisors by writing a few sentences about each and adding the participant's photo. On each page thereafter, write one question on the left side of the book and three or four answers on the right side. Include a photo of each respondent next to his or her answer so the learner can visualize who is giving each piece of advice.

Give this book to the student to study proactively or bring it out during confusing or frustrating moments. Add new pages as challenges emerge.

Consider adding the student's own voice to the book in spots. In other words, let the book serve as a tool for positive self-talk.

Example

A high school student with Asperger syndrome often consulted with classmates about personal struggles, such as how to cope with anxiety and how to deal with the pressures of school, including choosing a college and taking standardized tests. His teachers helped him to create a slam book filled with ideas from the classmates who he viewed as successful and trustworthy. His questions included, *How are you choosing a college?, How do you deal with anxiety during tests?, What do you do when you feel frustrated with a teacher over a grade?*

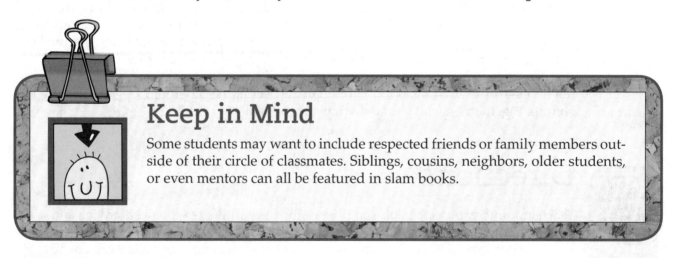

Keep in Mind

Some students may want to include respected friends or family members outside of their circle of classmates. Siblings, cousins, neighbors, older students, or even mentors can all be featured in slam books.

Reference

Hughes, C., & Carter, E. (2008). *Peer buddy programs for successful secondary school inclusion.* Baltimore, MD: Paul H. Brookes Publishing Co.

Vendor

Friendship Book

http://www.friendshipbook.com

This web site offers slam books for younger children with engaging pictures and fun getting-to-know-you questions.

Web Sites

eHow

http://www.ehow.com/how_2163255_slam-book.html

A short but useful tutorial on slam books.

Making Friends

http://www.makingfriends.com/slam_book.htm

Here you can find directions for making unique-looking slam books.

Teaching & Learning

Contents

51	Doughy Designs	122
52	Anchor Charts	125
53	Observation Bottles	128
54	Costumes	131
55	Off-the-Page Word Walls	133
56	Stick Puppets	136
57	Surprise Bags	138
58	Frisbee Toss	140
59	Pop-Ups	142
60	"All Done" Board	144

51 Doughy Designs

Materials

- 1 cup white flour
- 1 cup warm water
- 2 tbsp salt
- 2 tbsp cream of tartar
- 2 tbsp vegetable oil
- 1 3-oz pack of flavored gelatin

Description

Who didn't love playing with dough or modeling clay as a kid? When you bring these materials into the classroom, you will see that the urge to sculpt, pinch, stack, and build never ends. High school students will be as delighted as the little ones when you find reasons to roll out the dough. In addition, your sensory seekers will thrive when they are given a reason to knead and roll in the context of a standards-based lesson.

Dough and clay can be used in almost any subject area. For example, students can be charged with making the following:

- Atoms and molecules
- Land forms
- Continents
- The alphabet
- Leaf prints
- Phases of the moon
- Goods and services
- Free-standing sculpture
- Animal habitats
- Sets and subsets
- The solar system
- Story problems
- A story setting

Directions

Using a medium-sized sauce pan, mix the ingredients together and stir over low heat until your dough thickens into a ball. When you cannot stir anymore, the dough is done. Scoop it out of the pan and let it cool on a cutting board.

Once the dough can be handled, knead vigorously and add flour until it is no longer sticks to your hands.

The flavored gelatin will dye your dough, but if you want brighter colors, food coloring can be added at this time. Just make a dimple in the dough, drop in your coloring, and knead and fold until the color works its way through the ball. Repeat the process for each new color of dough you need to make. To save time and to build excitement for the upcoming classroom project, consider enlisting students to help with this step.

When you have achieved the color you desire, you are ready to use your dough and make your creations.

When students are finished using the dough, place it in an airtight container and store in the refrigerator. You should be able to keep using the same dough for a week or so.

Examples

A sixth-grade teacher had students create the atomic structures of carbon dioxide, water, and a sugar molecule using different colors of dough. Students took digital photographs of the models and posted them in their science notebooks as a study tool.

Students learning about the earth's crust, mantle, and core created mini-models of the planet using different colors of dough. Some students also created models of others planets to add to a model solar system.

Keep in Mind

Depending on what students are making, you may want to have a variety of supplies available for embellishing their creations such as craft sticks, small plastic toys, potato mashers, cookies cutters, toothpicks, muffin tins, leaves and twigs, rice and noodles, rolling pins, forks and spoons, and pipe cleaners.

References

Biel, L., & Peske, N. (2009). *Raising a sensory smart child: The definitive handbook for helping your child with sensory processing issues.* New York, NY: Penguin.

Caskey, P. (2006). *Make your own playdough, paint, and other craft materials: Easy recipes to use with young children.* St. Paul, MN: Redleaf Press.

Kohl, M. (2010). *Art with anything: 52 weeks of fun using everyday stuff.* Lewisville, NC: Gryphon House.

Vendor

Eco-Kids

http://www.ecokidsusa.com

Eco-Kids is a line of art supplies that are made using nontoxic, natural ingredients. In addition to dough, they offer paints, blocks, crayons, stickers, and glue.

Web Site

Play-doh

http://www.hasbro.com/playdoh

On Hasbro's site, you will find all things Play-doh, including ideas for creations and video tutorials.

52 Anchor Charts

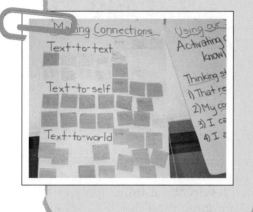

Materials

- Poster board or chart paper
- Markers
- Photographs

Description

Anchor charts are basically classroom posters containing key information, teachings, skills, or strategies. They are different from purchased posters in that they are dynamic; that is, they are created by and with students (often spontaneously) and they can grow throughout your day, your unit, or your year.

Anchor charts are so named because they are designed to help information stay "anchored" or stuck in students' minds. They can be used across subject areas. Although they are used often in elementary classrooms, they are just as appropriate for lessons in the upper grades. These visual supports serve many purposes. They certainly help students to learn material, but they also can increase student independence. Necessary information, such as *What do I capitalize?*, can be available in the room and unnecessary teacher questions can be avoided.

Further, anchor charts encourage student engagement and exploration of class materials. When learners see this prioritized content day in and day out, they begin to notice new examples and illustrations in their work that they might not have otherwise. If an anchor chart on assessing the reliability of information on the Internet is started, students might be inspired to add to it during WebQuests or after reading an article about the topic. For this reason, be sure to leave room on your charts for new contributions.

Directions

Decide on the focus for your anchor chart. To call your visual an anchor chart, it needs to have a single focus, such as the following:

- How to hook your reader
- How to partner read
- How to choose a book

- Rules for capitalization
- How to practice your scales
- How to hold your violin
- How to study for tests
- How to estimate
- When to use mean, median, or mode
- Examples of cardiovascular exercises
- What do we know about the brain?

Examples

An eighth-grade English teacher started an anchor chart to discuss symbolism in the texts the students were reading. She started the chart during a mini lesson about using symbolism in writing. Students shared examples to display on the chart. Throughout the year, new examples were added as learners discovered them in short stories, novels, and films.

A third-grade teacher started an anchor chart on creating a caring classroom after she observed students bickering with each other. Students generated a range of ideas and illustrated them as well. The class added to the chart throughout the year.

References

Diller, D. (2008). *Spaces & places: Designing classrooms for literacy.* Portland, ME: Stenhouse.

Dorfman, L.R., & Cappelli, R. (2009). *Nonfiction mentor texts: Teaching informational writing through children's literature, K–8.* Portland, ME: Stenhouse.

Harvey, S., & Goudvis, A. (2007). *Strategies that work: Teaching comprehension for understanding and engagement* (2nd ed.). Portland, ME: Stenhouse.

Vendor

Teachers Pay Teachers

http://www.teacherspayteachers.com

The best place to buy anchor chart templates is also the best place on the web to support fellow teachers. Just do a search for *anchor charts.*

Web Sites

Anchor Charts by Totally Incredible Teachers

http://totallyincredibleteachers.blogspot.com

An entire web site dedicated to sharing anchor charts.

Debbie Diller: A Journey in Learning

http://debbiediller.wordpress.com

Debbie Diller, a literacy and early learning expert, has a web site filled with ideas and photos. Page through her blog posts to find plenty of anchor chart ideas to use in your own classroom.

53 Observation Bottles

Materials

- Plastic bottles (e.g., peanut butter, water, shampoo)
- Beans or popcorn kernels
- Small objects related to content/lesson

Description

Observation bottles—clear containers designed to illustrate a concept or encourage play and experimentation—are inexpensive to make and provide a quick hands-on supplement to a lesson. For some students, certain discovery bottles also offer a sensory break because they can be intriguing and even mesmerizing to watch.

Some observation bottles encourage students to make predictions and solve problems. For example, a student looking at a rusting observation bottle might want to guess what the nuts and bolts will look like in 1 day, 3 days, or 2 weeks. A student looking at a letter tile bottle might estimate how many three-letter words could be created with the tiles he or she can see.

Observation bottles also can be fun community builders for the classroom. You can ask all students to bring in observation bottles containing objects that represent their life stories. The bottles could be shared in small groups and displayed in the classroom for a time.

Discovery bottles can also be considered tiny little experiments. They work well for students with disabilities because they create none of the mess that is usually associated with labs and experiments. In addition, there is no danger of ingesting materials. Furthermore, students interested in the concept you are teaching can take the bottle home and spend as much time exploring the materials as needed.

There are many types of observation bottles, including the following:

- *Math:* estimation challenge, number scramble (create number sentences with digits spotted), shape scramble (name or define shapes spotted), count and record (count identified objects; be sure that objects have different colors or shapes so learners know what has been counted and what has not been counted)

- *Literacy:* word/letter scramble (build words or sentences), toy/object scramble (write or tell stories using the first few objects found), ABC hunt (create bottles for each letter and let students take turns naming objects with the target letter)

- *Social studies:* desktop continent/state/region/city (identify words/phrase/objects related to each area), desktop land forms (create or study materials related to pond, lake, desert, etc.), desktop eras/time periods (create or study materials related to Industrial America, the Dark Ages, etc.)

- *Science:* magnetic illustration (add sand or rice, as well as a variety of magnetic items and nonmagnetic items; have students use a magnet on the outside of the bottle to see what it attracts and what it does not), rust illustration (add screws to the bottle and pour water over them so students can observe the process), tornado/vortex illustration (use water, salt, dish detergent, baking soda and food coloring to create a vortex in a bottle; small objects can be used to represent debris), density illustration (marbles or other objects are deposited into different materials such as water, gel, and sand), static illustration (add Styrofoam and tissue paper to the bottle and rub on clothing or carpet)
- *Languages:* see it and say it (use objects that represent vocabulary words and have students take turns finding objects and naming them in both languages)

Directions

Collect a large range of bottles. It will be easiest if you have the same bottles for the entire classroom so assembly is uniform and storage is easier.

Add materials to the bottle (e.g., nuts and bolts, magnets, letter tiles) and then add filler such as beads, pom-poms, hair gel, sand, confetti, or water if necessary. Add enough to fill the bottle completely.

Finish by using a hot glue gun to secure the lids on the bottles.

Use bottles during lab, at small group time, or as a centers activity or allow students to create their own as an experiment or discovery project.

Examples

Spanish II students used discovery bottles to practice new vocabulary words and to work on their conversational language skills. Working with a partner, students took turns commenting on something they found in the jar. So, the first student might say, "Veo dos tigres" ("I see two tigers"). The student's partner was then expected to respond and make a new statement about objects in the bottle. Different bottles were created for different units.

A middle school science teacher introduced one discovery bottle experiment per month. Each student made a bottle of his or her own and took them home to share with their families. The students were required to teach the concept (e.g., rusting, magnetism) to at least one person at home.

References

Arnwine, B. (2011). *Starting sensory therapy: Fun activities for the home and classroom.* Arlington, TX: Future Horizons.

Veenendall, J. (2008). *Arnie and his school tools: Simple sensory solutions that build success.* Shawnee Mission, KS: Autism Asperger.

Vendors

The Container Store

http://www.containerstore.com

Find the perfect jar or bottle for your materials.

Lakeshore Learning

http://www.lakeshorelearning.com/seo/ca\productSubCat~~p\AA931~~f\/Assortments/Lakeshore/ShopByCategory/infantstoddlers/viewall.jsp

These giant sight-and-sound tubes are great for little hands and are as fun as they are captivating. Some learners might enjoy the discovery aspect, whereas others will be thrilled with the sensory piece.

Oriental Trading

http://orientaltrading.com

Look here to find an assortment of small toys and craft supplies to use in the creation of your bottles.

Web Sites

Modern Parents Messy Kids

http://www.modernparentsmessykids.com/2011/11/we-tried-it-discovery-bottles.html

This web site is dedicated to finding ways to keep kids engaged and organized. This particular post offers an organized and simple way to look at discovery bottles.

Science Kids

http://www.sciencekids.co.nz

This site is a great resource not only for parents and teachers but for kids, too! Here you will find engaging science experiments, lesson plans, images, videos, and so much more to discover.

Steve Spangler

http://www.stevespangler.com

If you have not visited this blog, you are missing out on science teaching ideas galore. You will find a recipe for a "tornado in a bottle" and many other easy and impressive experiments and demonstrations.

54 Costumes

Materials

- Pieces of felt
- Old clothes
- Old hats
- Hoop skirts
- Capes
- Magic wands
- Hula hoops
- Fake beards
- Purses
- Sunglasses
- Neckties

Description

Make learning memorable in your classroom by adding a collection of outfits and props to your weekly lessons. Every student will enjoy and remember visits from notable figures, such as Amelia Earhardt, John Brown, Ivan the Terrible, and Cesar Chavez. They will also appreciate meeting "stars" of history (e.g., The Freedom Riders), darlings of literature (e.g., Tom Sawyer), amazing artists (e.g., Frida Kahlo), and great science minds (e.g., Marie Curie).

Remember the potential impact of moving beyond a person to a place or thing. The most creative teachers know how to whip up a Big Dipper costume, be a deciduous tree, become a First Amendment, or dress as a quarter note.

A day spent in a wig, cape, or waistcoat can have a lasting impact on any learner. Many students will remember your outfit and performance for months and even years, especially those learners who need to see or experience to remember or understand the material.

Directions

Page through your textbooks, scan classroom literature, and look to current events to choose your costumes. Keep in mind that your looks should help students better understand a person, place, time period, or concept so you might want to focus first on how to use costumes to improve comprehension. For example, co-teachers who dress like Union and Confederate soldiers help students immediately see the differences between battle dress today and in the past. Students will also quickly see why the sides are known as "the blue and the grey."

Helping students to deepen their understanding of a topic is not the only reason to use costumes, however. You also can use them to introduce a unit, spark interest in a lackluster topic, create laughter, inspire questions, and serve as a walking and breathing visual support for a lecture or discussion.

Examples

A fifth-grade teacher dressed up as a Midwestern homemaker from the 1800s to teach her unit on pioneers in America. She spent the day in a long flowered work dress and used props such as a butter churn, a dinner bucket, and a rag doll.

A middle school art teacher regularly dressed as famous artists and as subjects from well-known paintings. In a given year, she came to school as Mona Lisa, Whistler's Mother, and the Girl in the Pearl Earring. This was not only fun for students, but it made learning so memorable. She reported that students regularly told her that they saw "her painting" on television or that they researched her costume online.

Reference

Pogrow, S. (2008). *Teaching content outrageously: How to captivate all students and accelerate learning, Grades 4–12.* San Francisco, CA: Wiley.

Vendors

Costume Express
http://www.costumeexpress.com
This online shop has fantastic group costumes (e.g., Wizard of Oz) and some fun literary characters, too.

Wholesale Halloween Costumes
http://www.wholesalehalloweencostumes.com
There are many costumes to choose from on this web site, including Amelia Earhart, Ben Franklin, Medusa, and Teddy Roosevelt.

Web Site

Child Drama
http://www.childdrama.com
If you want to take your costume up a notch and add some drama, visit this web site for dozens of short plays and exercises.

55 Off-the-Page Word Walls

Materials

- Bulletin board paper
- Construction paper
- Stapler
- Plastic baggies
- Photographs
- Artifacts
- News clippings/articles

Description

Many students require alternative classroom materials. For them, learning and expressing learning is often easier when we abandon pencil and paper and get our lessons "off the page." For this reason and for these students, we started using and advocating for the use of off-the-page versions of classroom word walls.

Students without disabilities find these displays visually interesting and are constantly suggesting and adding new materials. Students with disabilities also enjoy finding new materials to add and they profit from being able to manipulate the materials displayed and physically explore the wall itself.

Three-dimensional walls are not only beneficial for students who are nonreaders but also for those who are blind or have low vision. Therefore, they are helpful tools in both the elementary and secondary classroom.

Directions

After you decide on your content area of focus, put your wall up with just a few terms and artifacts. Once students see the wall, invite them to make contributions. Create a formal time for this at first and then allow students to continue to make additions on their own.

Spend time each week interacting with your word wall. For younger students, interactions will likely be much more frequent. In secondary classrooms, even a few minutes once or twice a week may have an impact on student's acquisition of new words. You might start your week with a quick word wall activity, end each lesson with a question related to the wall, or incorporate a weekly game related to the terms and objects posted.

Once the wall is up, you will find many other ways to make it interactive, such as the following:

- *Engage in quick demonstrations on a regular basis.* Use the words in context, talk about how the words apply to daily lessons, and ask students to use the words as they talk about their work.

- *Play games.* For example, ask students to take turns hitting the wall with a beach ball. The term they hit is the one they have to define and explain.
- *Ask students to make contributions to the wall on a regular basis.* You might even make the addition of a term with related artifacts part of a homework assignment.
- *Ask students to work in teams to engage in "word wall theater."* Students can act out a word from the wall that you assign or a term that you pick from a hat.

Example

A high school math teacher creates interactive word walls for all of his classes. He invites students to create drawings, bring news clippings, and otherwise illustrate terms such as integer, polynomial, equation, coefficient, and slope. Every week, students complete a quick exercise related to the terms on the wall. They might, for instance, complete a KWL with a partner or they could be asked to make artifacts with group members that can be attached to the word wall.

Keep in Mind

If you lack space, use three-panel displays. These freestanding boards do not require any wall space, and they can be moved around the room and placed on a table for easy visibility and access.

References

Harmon, J.M., Wood, K.D., Hendrick, W.B., Vintinner, J., & Willeford, T. (2009). Interactive word walls: More than just reading the writing on walls. *Journal of Adolescent & Adult Literacy, 52,* 389–408.

Jackson, J., Tripp, S., & Cox, K. (2011). Interactive word walls: Transforming content vocabulary instruction. *Science Scope, 35*(3), 45–49.

Jasmine, J., & Schiesl, P. (2009). The effects of word walls and word wall activities on the reading fluency of first grade students. *Reading Horizons, 49,* 301–314.

Vendors

Have Fun Teaching
http://havefunteaching.com/tools/word-walls
Shop for word wall kits including those designed for science units.

Nasco

http://www.enasco.com/page/Math/math_FeaturedProducts0812

Visually appealing word cards for math word walls.

Web Sites

The Classroom Creative

http://www.theclassroomcreative.com/2012/08/28/word-wall-ideas

Over 20 creative ideas for K-12 word walls can be found on this blog.

Reading Rockets

http://www.readingrockets.org/strategies/word_walls

Reading Rockets is one of the best resources around for literacy ideas, including details on word walls.

56   Stick Puppets

Materials

- Craft sticks
- Glue
- Old books
- Magazines
- Large shoe or boot box

Description

When your books become tattered, do not throw them away. Instead, cut them up and create a series of stick puppets to use in retellings and dramatic play. The puppets can also be used as a tool for creating new narratives.

Puppets make lessons whimsical, bring a bit of levity to the classroom, and provide opportunities for writing, communication, and social interaction. These particular puppets have the added benefit of being really easy to make and having applications across grade levels.

Directions

Cut figures out of old books and magazines. People and animals obviously work well. Props will help students move their stories along, so be sure to include items such as houses, trees, and cars, too. If you cannot find the characters you need in books and magazines, have students draw characters on poster board and cut them out.

Using strong glue, mount each image on its own craft stick and let it dry thoroughly.

Provide students with an assignment related to their puppets. You might ask them to retell a story or act out a timeline from history, write a drama based on the characters they have created, practice new vocabulary words or language (e.g., alliteration, onomatopoeia).

If time and space permits, let students use book boxes or even trifold presentation boards to perform their puppet shows.

Example

Students in a ninth-grade English class had to make stick puppets and stick puppet theaters as part of their study of *Romeo and Juliet*. Each group had to choose a scene from the play, translate it into modern English, and act it out with puppets for the class. The scenes were shared chronologically so that the puppet shows resulted in a complete retelling of the play.

Reference

Kennedy, J.E. (2006). *Puppet planet: The most amazing puppet-making book in the universe.* Cincinnati, OH: North Light Books.

Vendors

Puppet Hut

http://www.puppethut.com

Stick puppets, glove puppets, finger puppets, and more are available on this site.

Shakespeare's Den

http://www.shakespearesden.com/mafipu.html

Here you can find unique items for your K–12 classroom, including puppets of Charles Dickens, Dorothy Parker, Charles Darwin, Queen Elizabeth, Marie Curie, Mahatma Gandhi, and even Pavlov's dog!

Web Sites

Dragons Are Too Seldom

http://www.dragonsaretooseldom.com/teach-puppets-math.html

Markie Scholz, one of the founders of Dragons Are Too Seldom Puppet Productions, has a web site filled with ideas for using puppets in the classroom, including this list on how to use puppets to teach math.

You and Me Puppets

http://www.youandmepuppets.com

Award-wining artist and educator, Judith O'Hare, has created a site on puppets that may interest both students and their teachers. It features resources on puppets and puppeteering. English, art, and drama teachers alike will find resources here.

57 Surprise Bags

Materials

- Paper bags
- Trinkets, toys, photographs, and other small objects

Description

Even the most trying of lessons can be made a bit more interesting by providing students with a secret bag of goodies. Surprise bags can be used to pique curiosity before a new unit or lesson, inspire innovation and creativity, and add a bit of humor or mystery to a potentially dry topic.

Directions

Provide individual students or small groups with a bag of objects. There are many ways to use the bags. You can hand them out as a writing prompt, then have students or small groups write a story that incorporates all of their objects into that story. You can give out bags before a unit starts and have students guess what the group will be studying. A teacher can provide students with artifacts, such as photos, magazines, letters, pieces of clothing, and maps, so that students can learn about a time period being studied. You can also collect materials that students can unpack and explore; in a science class, this might include a variety of rocks, objects found in nature, or even data collection instruments (e.g., different scales).

Examples

Every month, a creative writing teacher gave each one of her students a brightly colored bag filled with three to five objects. Every object in the bag had to be featured somewhere in the story. For example, a bag with a convertible, kitten, and a jump rope might lead a student to write about a magical driving cat who becomes the world's double-dutch champion.

A fifth-grade social studies teacher used surprise bags to build anticipation for upcoming units of study. When students were about to study the Oregon Trail, the bag was packed with a map of Oregon, a little plastic oxen and covered wagon, and a small white cloth sack with "gold" printed on the side. These objects were discussed before study of the topic began to ground learners in the most important elements of the unit, but they also served as visual supports for a student with multiple disabilities who benefitted from materials that made content less abstract and more concrete.

Keep in Mind

Students in upper grades may want to try stuffing some of the bags themselves. One homework assignment could be to bring in a filled bag to exchange with another learner.

References

Loomans, D., & Kolberg, K. (2002). *The laughing classroom: Everyone's guide to teaching with humor and play.* Tiburon, CA: Kramer.

Vendors

Steve Spangler Science
http://www.stevespanglerscience.com/category/be-amazing-toys
Many cool science toys and objects to explore.

Wonderbrains
http://www.wonderbrains.com
A variety of educational toys and games are available.

Web Site

Teachinghistory.org
http://teachinghistory.org/tah-grants/lessons-learned/23961
This post provides information on using artifacts in the social studies classroom.

58   Frisbee Toss

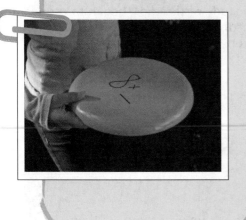

Materials

- Frisbee
- Dry erase marker

Description

Your physical education teacher may want to team up with you on this one. With the current push toward fitness and health in schools, many teachers are looking for teaching strategies that incorporate movement. This simple toss game serves as a vehicle for skills practice and as a way to get students running, jumping, throwing, and catching too.

Directions

Using a dry erase marker, write a category, math problem, or writing prompt on the top of the disc, then have students play Frisbee with a partner. Each time the Frisbee is caught, a response is required from that player. When students tire of a particular problem or category, they can wipe it off the Frisbee and record a new prompt or switch with another group of students.

Examples

On nice fall days, a third-grade class went outside for 10-minute segments to practice their multiplication tables. Students were put into partnerships with classmates with similar study needs. One pair might have a Frisbee with "9 × __" written on it and another pair might be practicing "1 × __."

An expository writing class played Frisbee toss to practice getting rid of trite expressions. Every time a student caught the disc, he or she had to call out an example of a cliché (e.g., *big as a house, sick as a dog*) and practice "tossing it" (by way of throwing the Frisbee) out of their writing.

Students in an American Government class were given time to play Frisbee as a review. Each student got a "cheat sheet" listing all of the amendments to the US Constitution. With each catch, students had to name an amendment and explain it. After several practice rounds, students tried to name amendments without looking at their sheets.

References

Jensen, E. (2008). *Brain-based learning: The new paradigm of teaching* (2nd ed.). Thousand Oaks, CA: Corwin Press.

Udvari-Solner, A., & Kluth, P. (2008). *Joyful learning: Active and collaborative learning in inclusive classrooms.* Thousand Oaks, CA: Corwin Press.

Vendors

Toys "R" Us

http://www.toysrus.com

Shop the site to find Frisbees of all shapes, colors, and sizes.

Motivators

http://www.motivators.com

If you want your Frisbees printed or branded, you can find a fairly large selection here.

Web Site

Classroom Game Nook

http://www.classroomgamenook.com

Rachel Parlett is an educator and classroom game enthusiast. Check out her site to find printables, freebies, and lots and lots of game ideas for your lessons.

59 Pop-Ups

Materials

- Origami papers
- Glue
- Scissors

Description

Many of our ideas are inspired by our former students with physical and multiple disabilities. We always had to look beyond traditional desktop activities to find materials students could feel, touch, and possibly manipulate. Therefore, when we discovered the possibilities for using these tactilely interesting three-dimensional figures across subject areas we knew we had to share them.

Pop-ups can be created by or for students. The sky is the limit when it comes to lesson ideas. Students can create pop-up bugs, power plants, flowers, Eiffel Towers, pyramids, and more.

Directions

Follow folding directions for your particular items. There are too many variations to describe here, so see the web site suggestions for step-by-step guidelines on different projects.

Once you have created your pop-ups, determine how you will use them. For example, do you want them to be used as part of a particular activity or can students explore them at any time?

Once you have displayed the pop-ups in the classroom, expect students to want to learn more about them. Again, use the suggested resources to teach students about how to make their own pop-up creations and pop-up books.

Example

A parent of a student with multiple disabilities was very artistic, so a middle school teacher asked for his help in making pop-ups that could be used in a discussion on architecture. The parent was pleased to be able to use his skills in his child's inclusive classroom, especially to create supports that were both visual and tactile and, therefore, perfect learning tools for his own child. This talented dad made an Eiffel Tower, a Roman coliseum, Egyptian pyramids, and even two Frank Lloyd Wright homes.

References

Birmingham, D. (2011). *Pop-up design and paper mechanics: How to make folding paper sculpture.* Indianapolis, IN: Wiley.

Ives, R. (2009). *Paper engineering and pop-ups for dummies.* Indianapolis, IN: Wiley.

Vendor

Creative Popup Cards

http://www.creativepopupcards.com/store

Visit this site to buy some great pop-up cards and to see a list of the 10 things you will need to create pop-ups (look under *Tools and Supplies*).

Web Sites

Free Kids Crafts

http://www.freekidscrafts.com/popups-t130.html

Easy tutorials on pop-ups are available here.

The Pop-Up Lady

http://www.popuplady.com

This talented artist is a writer, collector, curator, lecturer, and lover of pop-up and movable books.

Robert Sabuda

https://www.robertsabuda.com

Robert Sabuda's web site offers plenty of resources related to pop-ups, pop-up cards, and design.

Peter Dahmen

http://www.youtube.com/watch?v=yJwf-J84CjE

This video demonstrates the artist's beautiful paper engineering projects.

60 "All Done" Board

Materials

- Foam board, display board, or small bulletin board
- Sticky notes (different colors if possible)
- Markers or letter stickers

Description

There are so many benefits of having a differentiated classroom, but a challenge that may exist is managing the time and activities of your students. Although this is difficult in any classroom, in the differentiated classroom students may be using different materials, participating in different ways, and addressing different goals; therefore, the task may be even more onerous.

So, what is a teacher to do (especially one concerned about using every available minute of class time to teach and reach students)? One option is to create an "all done" choice board that incorporates multiple intelligences, features different subject areas, and can easily be changed from day to day, week to week, and month to month.

Directions

For this project, foam board seems to work best if you want your display to be portable and don't have a lot of extra space.

Somewhere at the top of the board, write or post a title so that students know the purpose of the board. They may panic until they see that these are not assignments for all, but choices for when they complete required assignments.

Generally, you can create four columns for language arts, math, social studies, and science. You can feature other areas of study within those categories so that you have choices related to art, music, technology, and other subjects, too.

Sticky notes are used to create choices. The use of sticky notes makes the options easy to switch out at any time. Options may stay up for the entire semester or they might change from week to week. You may choose to change only some options, keeping favorites (e.g., independent reading, exploring footage on the National Geographic web site) all year long.

Teachers in upper grades may have fewer choices because all options will relate to their subject area. Therefore, a math teacher may have only four options but rotate them regularly.

Example

Every minute seems to be differentiated in one sixth-grade classroom. Students not only experience novelty, choices, and challenge during assigned activities, but they can access an "all done" board when they finish their work. The core of the board stays the same all year, but new choices pop up regularly. Some of the choices include *write a chapter book, design a poster for our science fair,* and *visit one of our favorite math web sites.*

Reference

Tomlinson, C., & Imbeau, M. (2010). *Leading and managing a differentiated classroom.* Alexandria, VA: ASCD.

Vendor

Teachers Pay Teachers

http://www.teacherspayteachers.com/Browse/Search:choice+boards

Use this link to find choice boards and enrichment boards for just a few dollars (some are even free). This site is such a great way to support fellow teachers.

Web Sites

A Differentiated Kindergarten

http://www.differentiatedkindergarten.com

If you teach pre-K, kindergarten, first grade, or second grade, you will find plenty of ideas for your differentiated classroom here.

Differentiation Daily

http://www.differentiationdaily.com

On Paula's differentiation site for K–12 teachers, you will find plenty of resources to differentiate any subject area.

Literacy

Contents

61	Page Turners	148
62	Vocabulary Bars	150
63	Building Block Sentences	152
64	Story Stones	154
65	Slant Board	157
66	Story Starter Sticks	159
67	Word Exchange	162
68	Notebook Flipper	164
69	Poetry Dice	166
70	3D Venn Diagram	169

61 Page Turners

Materials

- Books
- Binder clips
- Craft sticks

Description

In some instances, differentiation is simply about making small changes to classroom materials. This is often the case, especially for learners with motor planning problems. These students might require a physical change to a book, for example, such as easy-to-manipulate page turners. Page turners can help students read more independently. They can also be used to help students find the most commonly used sections of text or reference books. This adaptation works well for board books and shorter texts.

Directions

Affix the craft sticks to the pages with glue and allow them to dry by spreading the book open and laying it on a flat surface.

For board books or texts that have thicker pages, binder clips can serve as impromptu and removable turners.

Examples

A social studies teacher created page turners for a few students with disabilities in his eighth-grade class. He used them for commonly referenced pages in his atlas, such as the glossary and the map of the world.

Students in a kindergarten class had access to hundreds of books on a range of topics, including many that were adapted for diverse learners. Some books had binder clip page turners, whereas others had craft stick page turners. Some of the books also had American Sign Language stickers affixed to help children learn new signs as they read.

References

Downing, J. (2005). *Teaching literacy to students with significant disabilities: Strategies for the K–12 inclusive classroom.* Thousand Oaks, CA: Corwin Press.

Erickson, K., & Koppenhaver, D. (2007). *Children with disabilities: Reading and writing the four-blocks way.* Greensboro, NC: Carson-Dellosa.

Kluth, P., & Chandler-Olcott, K. (2007). *A land we can share: Teaching literacy to students with autism.* Baltimore, MD: Paul H. Brookes Publishing Co.

Vendor

Enablemart

http://www.enablemart.com/computer-accessibility/furniture-and-accessories/book-holders-and-page-turners

Want a higher-tech page turner? Check out the many models offered here.

Web Site

Paths to Literacy

http://www.pathstoliteracy.org/modifying-books-students-multiple-disabilities

This site contains both original and reposted content related to literacy supports for students who are blind, visually impaired, or who have multiple disabilities. There are many useful posts on adapting instruction; this particular link will take you to several ideas for adapting text.

Pacer Center's Simon Technology Center

http://www.simontechnologycenter.blogspot.com

The Pacer Center's blog on assistive tech is outstanding. You will find simple low-tech ideas—such as how to create adapted books—as well as reviews of devices, apps, and software.

62 Vocabulary Bars

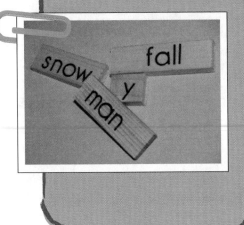

Materials

- Wood or tile pieces
- Letter stickers or marker

Description

One of the recommendations we make to teachers repeatedly is to "get it off the page." In other words, take typical paper and pencil tasks and create materials that are more interactive, novel, and appealing. Vocabulary bars certainly fall into this category. They provide students with a more tactile and active way to learn new vocabulary and to literally "play" with words as they try out prefixes, suffixes, compound words, and sentences.

Directions

To create bars, use materials you have on hand such as wood remnants, plastic cubes, or dominoes. Write directly on the bars or affix stickers to them. Choose words that students suggest as well as those prioritized in your units. You can create word bars and have students construct sentences, sentence predicates or subjects, or poems. Alternatively, you can have the learners focus on building words.

Example

Students in one second-grade class made their own vocabulary bar bags containing words they found interesting, in addition to words, suffixes, and prefixes provided by their teacher. Occasionally, students had opportunities to swap the words in their bags with classmates and acquire new ones for their personal collections.

References

Ganske, K. (2006). *Word sorts and more: Sound, pattern, and meaning explorations K–3.* New York, NY: Guilford.

Lubliner, S. (2005). *Getting into words: Vocabulary instruction that strengthens comprehension.* Baltimore: MD : Paul H. Brookes Publishing Co.

Vendors

Kaplan

http://www.kaplanco.com

High-frequency word tiles are available from Kaplan.

Nest Learning

http://www.nestlearning.com

On this web site, you can purchase 160 word tiles color coded by parts of speech.

Web Site

Merriam-Webster

http://visual.merriam-webster.com

Students can use this visual dictionary when learning new vocabulary and working on word sorts.

63 Building Block Sentences

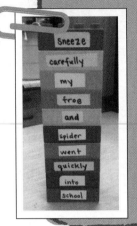

Materials

- Building blocks
- White stickers/labels

Description

Many students need "writing without a pencil" ideas in order to create letters, words, and sentences independently. If those same students happen to like playing with blocks, interlocking cubes, or building bricks, this teaching idea will be a hit.

Building block sentences allow students to link words together without having to form letters or think about spelling. Learners can stack and organize blocks to write phrases, sentences, and even short stories.

Directions

Using stickers (for small blocks) and sticker paper (for larger blocks), print words or letters you want students to use in their work. Affix one sticker to each block or brick.

You may let students make contributions at this point. They might each submit a favorite adjective (e.g., *squirrely*), a word related to a special interest (e.g., *locomotive*), or even their names.

Turn the final product over to students for free play or to complete certain activities. For example, the blocks might be at a learning center and students could be charged with creating a sentence with at least three words.

Example

Fourth-grade students used building blocks to form sentences at one of the literacy centers in their classroom. They were given new challenges every week, such as forming a compound sentence, an interrogative sentence, or a sentence with an independent clause. Then, they photographed their sentences with a digital camera to share with other groups.

References

Johnson, J.A., & Johnson, T.A. (2006). *Do-it-yourself early learning: Easy and fun activities and toys from everyday home center material*. St. Paul, MN: Redleaf Press.

MacDonald, S. (2001). *Block play*. Beltsville, MD: Gryphon House.

O'Connor, R.E. (2007). *Teaching word recognition: Effective strategies for students with learning disabilities*. New York, NY: Guilford Press.

Southhall, M. (2007). *Differentiated literacy centers: 85+ leveled activities with reproducible planning sheets and student pages to support centers in fluency, reading, comprehension, and word study*. New York, NY: Scholastic.

Vendors

Lakeshore Learning

http://www.lakeshorelearning.com

You can find foam blocks, cardboard blocks, wooden blocks, interlocking cubes (manipulatives), and more.

LEGO

http://www.lego.com

Shop here for all things LEGO.

Reading Manipulatives

http://www.readingmanipulatives.com

Other literacy-related manipulatives to use in K–8 classrooms are available.

Web Site

LEGO Education

http://www.legoeducation.com

This part of the LEGO site contains many ideas for bringing design and innovation into the classroom. There are language arts, science, and art ideas for all ages.

64 Story Stones

Materials

- Smooth rocks or stones
- Pieces of felt, cloth, or paper, paint, or markers
- Glue sealer (e.g., Mod Podge)

Description

Stones have been used in different cultures through the years to document experiences, pass stories across time and groups, and express ideas. This literacy tool not only builds on this history, but it allows learners to invent and engage in a unique and tactilely interesting way.

There are countless ways to use stones in the classroom. You can explore storytelling and engage in mini lessons about providing details, creating dialogue, and retelling by using nothing more than these little canvases.

Directions

To create the stones, you can use many different types of materials. You can create simple line drawings with a marker, or paint with acrylics, glue on fabric, or even sketch with chalk.

To be sure that you will be able to use your stones for many different purposes, you will want to include both nouns and verbs (either by making word stones or by showing symbols related to actions), plenty of possible characters and settings, numbers and math symbols, and perhaps even pictures related to content area vocabulary (e.g., desert , minutemen, vertex, protozoa).

No matter what materials you use, be sure to preserve your artwork by painting over your art with a glue, sealant, or varnish. After adding a coat or two, let the stones dry for a few hours.

When you are ready to use story stones with students, begin the lesson by modeling what you want them to do. Consider these lesson and activity possibilities:

- If you have multiples of certain pictures, have students "write" story problems (e.g., two cookies plus two cupcakes equals four treats).

- Have peer partners practice vocabulary words by selecting stones and defining what they see (e.g., hexagon, arachnid).
- Have students write sentences for themselves or for partners using the stones. Then, have the students use these sentences to start a story.
- Challenge your learners to pick three stones from a bag (without peeking) and write a 10-minute poem using all three ideas/images.
- Using stones specially created for this purpose, have students engage in a retelling using story stones that feature specific characters, events, settings, and details from a novel, short story, or picture book.
- Have students write collaborative stories as a community-building exercise. Each student in a small group selects a stone and adds one sentence to an ongoing story. This can even be played with the whole class.
- Use story stones as mystery writing prompts. Have students select a stone and write in a designated genre (e.g., ghost story, top-10 list, haiku, song lyrics, business letter, letter to the editor, speech).

 # Examples

Students with disabilities in one kindergarten class have the choice of retelling read-alouds with or without their story stones. Students who are particularly skilled are often encouraged to try the task without stones, but others are encouraged to use the props until they can be more successful without visuals.

In an eighth-grade English class, students were assigned a writing exercise every Friday. They worked on this piece of writing for an entire class period. They were assessed on different skills each week. One week the focus might be on figurative language and another week the target skill could be using memorable adjectives. Students were instructed to focus on the new skill or competency in their writing, but they were allowed some freedom in choosing a topic. Sometimes the teacher let students engage in a free write, where they could select any topic. Other times he asked them to generate a topic idea and then trade it with a partner. Still other times he asked students to choose a story stone from a coffee can filled with more than 50 stones. Pictures on the stones varied from a steam engine to Egypt to a zombie.

Keep in Mind

You can also introduce story stones as a purposeful fidget of sorts. These tiny, shiny pieces of art can serve as worry rocks or even as sensory-friendly manipulatives.

References

Hodgdon, L.A. (2011). *Visual strategies for improving communication: Practical supports for autism spectrum disorders.* Troy, MI: Quirk Roberts.

Klingner, J.K., Vaughn, S., & Boardman, A. (2007). *Teaching reading comprehension to students with learning difficulties.* New York, NY: Guilford Press.

Richard, E. (2005). *10 reading comprehension card games: easy-to-play, reproducible card and board games that boost kids' reading skills and help them succeed on tests.* New York, NY: Scholastic.

Vendor

Rory's Story Cubes

http://www.storycubes.com

These little cubes may not be personalized in the way that your own story stones are, but they are a quick and easy substitute. Visit the site not only to purchase cubes, but to read stories others have created based on their cube shakes.

Web Sites

ReadWriteThink

http://readwritethink.org

Countless reading activities and tools, including many designed for visual learners, can be found on this web site sponsored by the International Reading Association and the National Council of Teachers of English.

Use Visual Strategies

http://www.usevisualstrategies.com

This is Linda Hodgdon's professional web site. She does indeed sell her book and related products on the site, but she also has plenty of free tips and information.

65 Slant Board

Materials

- 3-inch three-ring binder
- Clipboard
- Glue gun
- Hook-and-loop tape

Description

Slant boards are an uncomplicated piece of assistive technology that can make reading and school work more accessible for a wide range of learners. A book or worksheet placed on a slant board at the correct angle can help students gain control of their writing and reading materials; reduce eye strain (because the eyes do not have to keep refocusing as the student progresses down the page); reduce the possibility of muscle fatigue; help students focus on their own work (especially those sitting at a table with a small group); allow the student to write more clearly; and encourage a healthier posture and, therefore, a healthier spine.

Directions

Create your board by gluing your binder to the clipboard or securing it with two or three rows of hook-and-loop tape. Then, decorate your binder with duct tape or colorful stickers or let the student decorate if you want to personalize the board and make it a bit more appealing for the learner to use.

If you want to be sure that the board stays in place, you can also use hook-and-loop tape to secure the binder to a table or desk. This way, when the board is not in use, the learner can use the spiky tape as a desktop fidget.

Allow the student to use the board when necessary. It might be used for reading or writing tasks. Students may also want to use their boards for certain art projects.

Examples

A middle school art teacher, noticing how beneficial a slant board was to one of her students with cerebral palsy, promptly acquired several more to use in her classes and offered them to any artist who wanted an alternative surface for drawing or painting.

An occupational therapist offering push-in support in a first-grade classroom provided a slant board to a student with Down syndrome and a few other learners without identified needs during morning journal time.

Reference

Orlich, D.C., Harder, R.J., Callahan, R.C., Trevisan, M.S., Brown, A., & Miller, D. (2013). *Teaching strategies: A guide to effective instruction* (10th ed.). Boston, MA: Cengage Learning.

Vendors

Therapro
http://www.therapro.com
Inexpensive slant boards of different sizes and colors can be found here.

Visual Edge
http://www.visualedgesb.com
The Visual Edge offers lots of different slant board products and related accessories (e.g., paper clips, book catch).

Web Site

The Recycling Occupational Therapist
http://recyclingot.blogspot.com
This talented OT has so many ideas for repurposing household items to create assistive technology and sensory supports. She uses lots of photos and step-by-step directions so you can easily create the projects she features.

66 Story Starter Sticks

Materials

- Craft sticks in different colors (or you can paint them)
- Marker
- Three small buckets, baskets, or cups

Description

Many students struggle to get started when they have to engage in independent writing tasks. Some overthink their plot or problem ideas and cannot think of just one. Some students use the same characters or themes repeatedly and do not like to move out of their comfort zone. Others just need something different to get motivated and to stay motivated during writing tasks.

Story starters can help students with any one of these challenges, but they can also be fun to use in lessons that might be a bit dull. For example, if you need students to write stories using details or rich dialogue, have them use story starter sticks so they can get started quickly and focus on the target skill instead of on character, setting, or problem decisions.

Directions

Separate craft sticks by color and label one bucket "character," one "setting," and one "plot". Write different ideas on each craft stick and put them in the appropriate containers.

For young learners, you will want to create story starter sticks for your students. For those in Grades 2–12, however, it can be fun to design with your learners.

Examples of characters include robot, spy, mermaid, wizard, frog, villain, Snow White, superhero, gingerbread man, old man, submarine captain, football fan, noisy baby girl, small-town mayor, fastest man on earth, talking dog, social worker, and shark hunter. Examples of settings include vacant lot, Panama, the base of the Statue of Liberty, remote beach, raft in the middle of the ocean, magical zoo, street corner, inside a television, Saturn, a living room in Iowa in 1970, and a haunted classroom. Examples of problems include not being able to find a treasured object, being thirsty all day every day, losing the ability to say words that contain the letter *A*, getting lost, ruining something valuable, not being able to wake from a dream, trying to fix a broken time machine, and making the neighbors mad.

To use the sticks, you can let students browse the choices at a writing station or center. Alternatively, you can pass them out randomly before an assignment. In this version, you would toss one stick from each cup on each learner's desk. Students are then asked to create stories based on these prompts.

Examples

A fifth-grade teacher had every student in her classroom make a set of story starter sticks (one for each category). Students signed their sticks on the back so that users could see who submitted each character, plot, and problem. Throughout the year, when students used the sticks for journal writing or for writing workshop, they would have fun seeing which sticks they chose and which classmates created them.

A high school Spanish teacher used story starter sticks to have her students write short stories of one or two paragraphs. This exercise forced them to use or learn new vocabulary words not typically taught in daily lessons (e.g., wizard) and helped them practice written language skills.

References

Harris, K.R., Graham, S. Mason, L. & Friedlander, B. (2008). *Powerful writing strategies for all students.* Baltimore, MD: Paul H. Brookes Publishing Co.

Stanek, L. (2003). *Story starters: How to jump-start your imagination, get your creative juices flowing, and start writing your story or novel.* New York, NY: Quill.

Vendor

McDonald Publishing

http://www.mcdonaldpublishing.com/p-516-story-starters-write-abouts-4-8.aspx

You can find several different version of story starter "write abouts" from this publisher. The first section of these three-part flip books contains exciting quotations. The second section identifies a character (e.g., the person responsible for the quotation), and the last section contains situations in which you might hear the quotations.

Web Sites

Creative Writing Now

http://www.creative-writing-now.com

Free story starters, creative writing ideas, and cures for writer's block are included.

Scholastic

http://www.scholastic.com/teachers/story-starters

This resource allows children to generate a creative story starter online, pick a format for their story, and print their work.

The Story Starter

http://thestorystarter.com

Created by Joel Heffner, this web site is a one-click solution for those students who say, "I don't know what to write about!" On every visit, you can create dozens or hundreds of unique story starters, such as, "The funny optometrist destroyed the evidence in the ballroom to quiet the angry mob."

67 Word Exchange

Materials

- Paper
- Laminator
- Library book pockets, small buckets, or hanging shoe organizer with multiple pockets

Description

Many English and language arts teachers try to teach students to use language that is powerful and interesting. Many teach the mantra *said is dead*, meaning that students need to expand the verbs they use in their writing. Instead of *said*, students might be encouraged to use *exclaimed, wondered,* or *whispered*. Getting students to use a wider range of words may be a challenge, however.

The interactive word exchange comes in handy for this purpose. It provides students with a visual they can access daily to remind them of the most commonly overused words. Further, this support allows students to physically interact with potential word choices, which is often appreciated by those who like to take their work off the written page and use new and different types of learning materials.

Directions

Start by identifying the words your students use too often (e.g., beautiful, big, good, great, happy, hot, important, interesting, little, mad, old, sad, scared). Then create your visual. You can staple library book pockets to a board, hang tiny buckets, or use a shoe organizer with ample space for multiple words.

To introduce your exchange, you might design a lesson where students create words to add to the existing options on the wall. Alternatively, you could arrange a learning station where students have to revise a piece of writing using the words on the exchange.

After students have been introduced to the exchange, you can encourage them to visit it on their own during a writing task or during the process of revision.

Example

A high school English teacher used a word exchange to teach and reinforce vocabulary words (e.g., acute, demean, extol). She not only encouraged students to use the exchange on their own during writing assignments, but designed activities around the word cards. For example, she would distribute a word to each student and have them find a partner who was holding a synonym.

References

Bear, D.R., Invernizzi, M., Templeton, S., & Johnston, F. (2004). *Words their way: Word study for phonics, vocabulary and spelling instruction (3rd ed.).* Upper Saddle River, NJ: Pearson Education.

Bromely, K. (2002). *Stretching students' vocabulary: Best practices for building the rich vocabulary students need to achieve in reading, writing, and the content areas.* New York, NY: Scholastic.

Carleton, L., & Marzano, R.J. (2010). *Vocabulary games for the classroom.* Bloomington, IN: Marzano.

Vendor

The Library Store

http://www.thelibrarystore.com/category/book_pockets

Inexpensive and colorful library pockets are available.

Web Site

VocabularySpellingCity

http://www.spellingcity.com

This award-winning web site is dedicated to helping students, teachers, parents, and school systems. Their mission is to provide "efficient game-based study of literacy skills."

68 Notebook Flipper

Materials

- Index card spiral notebook
- Scissors
- Marker

Description

Many educators (and parents) use flashcards to teach children early reading skills. Although literacy instruction must consist of much more than word work, flashcards are a nice supplement to a balanced literacy program; they provide opportunities for repeated practice, they can be used in one-on-one or tutoring sessions or in small groups, and they are an ideal "sponge" for absorbing the first few or last few minutes of a class period.

If you have students who have tired of the "same old, same old" and crave something new in their word work, then try notebook flippers. They have a dynamic quality that is missing from traditional flashcard work. Further, they can be easily created by teachers or students.

Using these pocket-sized books, students can learn sight words, spelling patterns, phoneme substitution, rhyming words, word families, and blends and digraphs.

Directions

After you cut the notebook into the number of sections that you want, label each card or page with a letter. You can also add some blends to your sections (e.g., instead of the letter *t*, you could use *th*).

You will quickly see that not all of the words formed are actually words! However, this is part of the fun of the book. If your focus is on learning sounds, it is fine to work on sounding out nonsense words—after all, that is how Dr. Seuss made a living. Furthermore, asking students to read nonsense words is one way to assess their abilities to blend letters into words when they do not know the word by sight.

If you want to add to the challenge or shake the activity up a bit, you can ask students to find and read at least 10 "real" words and 10 nonsense words. Or you can play an active response game in which students stand when they see a nonsense word and stay seated when they see a real word. This game can help with vocabulary for very young readers because it will bring up discussions about what it means to *flop* or what a *bin* is.

Students can use the notebook flippers alone or with partners. Students can be given time to practice their words, quiz their classmates, and "write" without using a pencil. You can give different books to different students to differentiate practice sessions.

Example

A kindergarten teacher gave one of her students "flipper work" as a regular homework assignment. Because the student struggled to fill in worksheets and complete word work on the page, the teacher sent home his notebook flipper at least once a week and assigned him to practice for 10 minutes with a parent, sibling, or stuffed animal.

References

Hall, D.P., & Cunningham, P.M. (2008a). *Making words first grade: 50 interactive lessons that build phonemic awareness, phonics, and spelling skills.* Upper Saddle River, NJ: Pearson.

Hall, D.P., & Cunningham, P.M. (2008b). *Making words kindergarten: 50 interactive lessons that build phonemic awareness, phonics, and spelling skills.* Upper Saddle River, NJ: Pearson.

Henry, M.K. (2003). *Unlocking literacy: Effective decoding and spelling instruction.* Baltimore, MD: Paul H. Brookes Publishing Co.

Vendor

Lakeshore Learning

http://www.lakeshorelearning.com

Browse several different flipbooks on this teacher-friendly site. You can buy sets for an entire class and you can choose from either word family flipbooks or phonics flipbooks.

Web Site

Fun 4 the Brain

http://www.fun4thebrain.com/English/popcornWords./html

You can be sure students will like a web site with *fun* in its name. This link will take you directly to a game called Popcorn Words, which features dozens of the most common sight words, but all of this interactive and engaging site will captivate your young learners.

69 Poetry Dice

Materials

- Tissue boxes
- Tag board or paper
- Markers

Description

Add an element of chance to your writing instruction with poetry dice. These easy-to-create die can feature any kind of content you choose and can be used to teach poetry, parts of speech, use of details, genre, figurative language, vocabulary words and more.

Directions

To make the dice, create 12 prompts, categories, or ideas. Print each of these out or write them on tag board and affix one to each side of the two die. Each die should have a different theme and different content. For instance, one might feature types of poems (e.g., haiku, sonnet, limerick). The other die can include topics (e.g., elephants, anger, birthday cake). Students can then roll the dice to get an assigned topic (e.g., a haiku about birthday cake).

Give one pair of dice to each group of students. Have them create products based on their rolls. Ideas for dice include the following:

- Types of poems and topics
- Types of poems and potential first lines
- Types of poems and metaphors to include
- Types of stories and a line of dialogue that must be included
- Types of stories and title ideas
- Types of stories and characters to include
- Types of essays and topics

Examples

A German teacher used dice to challenge her students to use new vocabulary words. Each die featured words in German. One die contained the names of people or subjects (e.g., dog, uncle) and the other included descriptions (e.g., tall, innocent, red). Students took turns shaking the dice and talking about the topic they rolled (e.g., the innocent dog).

English students worked with partners to write epic poems using topics they rolled on classroom dice. One student wrote a poem about an accountant on the Appalachian Trail and another had the charge of creating one featuring a German Shepherd on Saturn.

Students in a sixth-grade classroom used their dice as a way to boost the participation of a student with cognitive disabilities. The student learned how to use his new communication device by commenting on the topics he rolled or those that his peers rolled. The comments that were placed on his board included good roll, that one is ridiculous, you should really roll again, and somebody give me a first line for my poem.

References

Chatton, B. (2010). *Using poetry across the curriculum: Learning to love language* (2nd ed.). Santa Barbara, CA: Libraries Unlimited.

Corbett, P. (2008). *Poetry: Games and activities for ages 7–12.* New York, NY: Routledge.

Janeczko, P.B. (2011). *Reading poetry in the middle grades: 20 poems and activities that meet the Common Core Standards and cultivate a passion for poetry.* Portsmouth, NH: Heinemann.

Vendors

Great Extensions

http://www.great-extensions.com/dice5.html

You can reinvent this activity across subject areas and grade levels after exploring this site, where you will find dice featuring letters, words, animals, numbers, fractions, continents, and months of the year.

Story Cubes

http://www.storycubes.com

The dice in this popular tabletop game are filled with pictures that can inspire poems, stories, essays, and jokes.

Web Sites

ReadWriteThink

http://readwritethink.org/materials/bio_cube

This is a neat activity for kids and adults alike! Students fill in sides of a cube, entering information such as name, background, and biggest obstacle. The activity is typically used as a comprehension tool for exploring main characters or for learning about an individual before or after reading an autobiography, but it can just as easily be used by students as a tool for sharing about themselves.

Poetry for Children

http://poetryforchildren.blogspot.com

Sylvia Vardell is a professor and author of the bestseller *Poetry Aloud*. Her blog is filled with resources related to poetry for children.

Poets.org

http://www.poets.org

This is a must-visit web site for teachers and their young poets. You will find poems, ideas for teaching poetry, book reviews, essays, and information on National Poetry Month.

70　3D Venn Diagram

Materials

- Two hula hoops
- Markers
- Notecards
- Objects relevant to your lesson

Description

Venn diagrams normally comprise overlapping circles. The interior of the circle symbolically represents the elements of the set, while the exterior represents elements that are not members of the set. For example, in a two-set Venn diagram, one circle may feature themes from one coming-of-age novel, *The Lord of the Flies,* whereas the other might represent themes from *The Hunger Games.* The content in the intersecting area represents themes common to both texts (e.g., survival).

Even students in the earliest grades are familiar with Venn diagrams, so getting them interested in the creation of yet another graphic organizer can be a challenge. One way to make the task a bit more interesting is to offer students the opportunity to create a three-dimensional diagram on their own or with partners. Many students find the oversized visual fun to use and others enjoy the task because it provides a bit of movement and interaction. This format profits students with fine motor struggles. Students with disabilities can place stickers or signs inside the diagram instead of having to write individual words or phrases.

Directions

First, have students create their diagrams on paper. Then, hand out the hula hoops and let them fill in their diagrams on a flat surface. You could also tape or otherwise mount the hoops on the walls or board.

Give students time to "tour" the classroom and examine the diagrams created by peers.

Examples

In one middle school science class, students used three-dimensional Venn diagrams to compare ecosystems. Every pair of students compared two different ecosystems and then shared their diagram with several other groups.

A fifth-grade social studies teacher took his students outside to create three-dimensional Venn diagrams on the sidewalk. He gave each small group two hula hoops and sidewalk chalk and asked them to create diagrams comparing and contrasting George Washington and Abraham Lincoln.

A classroom of first graders worked together to create a 3-D Venn diagram of North American and Australian animals. Students used word cards and stuffed toys in their creation.

Keep in Mind

Objects can also be used to create three-dimensional Venn diagrams. This version will work well for students who are emerging readers or for those learning English. It can also be used as a unique alternative to written work for any student. You might, for instance, have students compare symbolism used in two different books. Instead of asking learners to express that content in words, ask them to bring in objects to represent the symbols. So, to use the example of the two novels shared earlier, students might bring in eyeglasses, a conch, and a model airplane for *The Lord of the Flies*. For *The Hunger Games*, students might bring dandelions, food/bread, and a toy television. A photograph of a fire might be a symbol placed in the intersection of the two circles.

References

Barnekow, D. (2009). *3-D graphic organizers: 20 innovative, easy-to-make learning tools that reinforce key concepts and motivate all students*. New York, NY: Scholastic.

McKnight, K.S. (2010). *The teacher's big book of graphic organizers: 100 reproducible organizers that help kids with reading, writing, and the content areas*. San Francisco, CA: Jossey-Bass.

Vendors

Discounted School Supply

http://www.discountschoolsupply.com

Search for *activity hoops* and choose from a selection of hula hoops and similar equipment.

Ward's Science

http://sciencekit.com/venn-diagram/p/IG0029410

This company offers a kit consisting of an oversized Venn diagram and 23 pockets that can be filled with any words or phrases appropriate for your organizer.

Web Site

A Periodic Table of Visualization Methods

http://www.visual-literacy.org/periodic_table/periodic_table.html#

From area charts to mindmaps to story templates, this impressive table provides examples of nearly every visual support you can imagine. Use it to move beyond Venn diagrams and consider other organizers that might be made into three-dimensional models.

Mathematics

Contents

71 Foldables 174

72 Interactive Bulletin Boards 176

73 Numbers Alive 178

74 Graph Guides 180

75 Sticky Sticks 182

76 Cardboard Dominoes. 184

77 Recycled Keyboard. 186

78 Wipe-Off Flashcards. 188

79 Checkerboard Review 190

80 Student-to-Student Tutorials 192

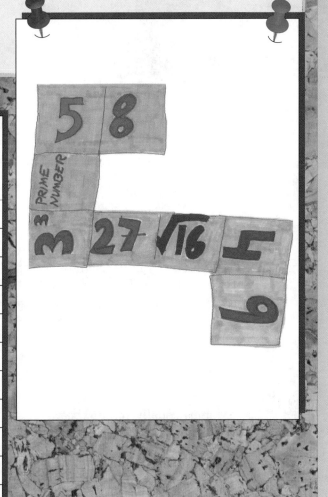

71 Foldables

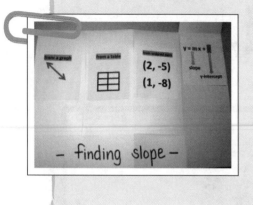

Materials

- Construction paper
- Paper
- Markers

Description

Foldables are three-dimensional, graphic organizers that allow students to display their learning in a memorable way. Foldables often appeal to visual and kinesthetic learners and can even serve as a "fidget" of sorts for those who do better with interactive materials.

Foldables can be used to teach and study any idea, concept, person, place, event, theory, or question. They can be used for note taking, journaling, diagramming, comparing and contrasting, displaying data sequencing, and concept or story mapping. Foldables can serve as assessments, study guides, self-guided learning tools, or even tutoring supports.

Directions

Foldables usually require between one and four pieces of paper. Depending on the foldable, you may use white or manila construction paper or any array of colored pages.

Students will need specific directions for both the folding of the product and the adding or displaying of content. Older learners can follow a step-by-step written checklist. For younger children, however, you will want to construct the foldable itself as a class so important directions are not missed.

Once students have created their product, you can have them revisit the foldable and review the content regularly. You can also have students use them with partners as study tools.

Examples

An algebra teacher uses a basic three-door foldable to teach set notation. The first flap contains all of the information about set notation, the second flap features algebraic notation, and the third flap focuses on interval notation.

Every student in a middle school math class made a "shutter fold" organizer to compare acute and obtuse angles. These foldables open like shutters so that students can include information on two sides of a page, but open one flap at a time to read about only one topic or the other. Every student had to research each topic and include information he or she felt was most important to the unit of study. One student with Down syndrome, however, was responsible for drawing one angle on each side, but primarily used pre-printed content provided by a teacher. The goal for this student, then, was not to create his learning tool independently, but to learn the facts provided.

Keep in Mind

Foldables can be used in any subject area: science, health, physical education, music, art, consumer education, social studies, and language arts. For example, during a study of prefixes, a fourth-grade teacher had her students create eight-flap foldables. Each flap featured a prefix on the outside (e.g., *auto-*, *ante-*). Under the flap, students wrote the meaning of the prefix and three words with the given prefix.

References

Barnekow, D. (2009). *3-D graphic organizers: 20 innovative, easy-to-make learning tools that reinforce key concepts and motivate all students!* New York, NY: Scholastic.

Zike, D. (2009). *Foldables, notebook foldables, & VKVs for spelling and vocabulary 4th–12th.* San Antonio, TX: Dinah-Might Adventures.

Vendor

Teachers Pay Teachers

http://www.teacherspayteachers.com

The best place to buy templates for foldables is also the best place on the web to support fellow teachers. Just do a search for *foldables.*

Web Site

Dinah Zike

http://www.dinah.com

Dinah Zike is an expert on the topic of using foldables in the classroom. She has written many books on the topic, offers workshops on the subject, and offers many ideas on her professional site.

72 Interactive Bulletin Boards

Materials

- Roll of paper
- Construction paper
- Sticky notes, library pockets, and hook-and-loop tape
- Display board or bulletin board

Description

Most teachers are required to create informative or inspiring bulletin boards for their classrooms. Why not use your wall space a bit differently and provide yet another opportunity for learning in your differentiated classroom. Interactive bulletin boards are a self-teaching and self-correcting tool for students and allow them to learn new things at their own pace and in their own way. You can add worksheets or exit slip questions and use these for a quick assessment if you want to enhance the experience.

Directions

Examine your curriculum and look for concepts or ideas that you would like to emphasize and reinforce. Create your board using hidden panels, hook-and-loop tape, magnets, erasable writing surfaces, sticky notes, or paper pockets to provide students opportunities to manipulate the materials.

Explain the rules of the board to the class. Consider at least the following questions: Is this a board that offers challenge problems only? Do you record answers on the board or submit them to the teacher? Can you use the board anytime or only after independent work is completed? Should you leave evidence of your work during each visit (e.g., a signed sticky note with a response)? Is it just for fun? Are there different ways for different students to play?

Examples

A "mean, median, and mode" bulletin board was created for students in a fifth-grade math class. The board consisted of several hands of playing cards. The objective was for students to calculate the mean, median, and mode of each hand. Students could fill out an answer form each week and enter a classroom contest where the goal was to submit an answer sheet with a perfect score. The board was posted for three weeks and students could enter each week. Prizes included math-themed playing cards and Sudoku puzzle books.

An interactive bulletin board was created during a fractions unit in a third-grade classroom. The teacher posted a fraction every few days. Students were invited to use sticky notes to add story problems with the featured fraction as the solution to the problem.

Keep in Mind

Teachers often think of interactive bulletin boards as tools for elementary school classrooms, but they also can be very useful in secondary classrooms—especially when they are changed often. They can inspire rich classroom discussions and serve as an enrichment tool as well.

References

Meagher, J., & Novelli, J. (1999). *Interactive bulletin boards: Math.* New York, NY: Scholastic.
Partin, R.L. (2009). *The classroom teacher's survival guide: Practical strategies, management techniques, and reproducibles for new and experienced teachers.* San Francisco, CA: Jossey Bass.

Vendor

US Markerboard

http://www.usmarkerboard.com

You do not need large wall-mounted bulletin boards for every interactive activity. On this site, you can find all sizes of boards, including some that would work well on tabletops and in smaller nooks and corners.

Web Site

Bulletin Boards to Remember

http://bulletinboardstoremember.blogspot.com

This blogging art teacher features post after post of gorgeous bulletin boards she finds on the Internet.

73 Numbers Alive

Materials

- Colored paper
- Sheet protector
- Marker

Description

This activity is a fun way to get students moving and help them to understand how numbers work before they rush to "solve the problem." Your social students, your lovers of play and drama, and your kinesthetic learners will likely all be fans of numbers alive.

Directions

Using brightly colored paper, draw or print one number on each page. Using another color of bright paper, create the symbols necessary for your equations (+, –, =). Call students up to the front of the room to represent parts of the equation or number.

In teaching turnaround facts (the commutative property), sentences can be formed by having each student hold an addend or a symbol. Then, to demonstrate how addends can be switched to get the same sum, you can have the students holding the two addend signs switch places. Each time, have observers chant the new equation. In a more complex equation, you can demonstrate the order of operations. Just have students step forward as their part of the problem is discussed. You can also use this activity to create numbers. Just use commas to show place value, adding students slowly to grow the number.

Examples

In a first-grade classroom, the teacher gave every student a number or symbol. Then, she called out number sentences and had students run to get into their designated places. Once the "team" was in place, all students chanted out the number sentence together. Occasionally students raced against each other by working in teams.

A similar game was used to teach second graders the concept of "greater than" and "less than." Two students held symbol cards while other classmates took turns serving as 3, 4, and 5 digit numbers. As students watching called out "greater than" or "less than" with each comparison, the student with the correct symbol would jump into place.

References

Allsopp, D., Kyger, M. & Lovin, L. (2007). *Teaching mathematics meaningfully: Solutions for reaching struggling learners.* Baltimore, MD: Paul H Brookes Publishing Co.

Kemp, K., Eaton, M.A., & Poole, S. (2009). *RTI and math: The classroom connection.* New York, NY: National Professional Resources.

Vendor

Montessori for Everyone

http://www.montessoriforeveryone.com/Large-Small-Number-Decimal-Cards_p_122.html

Check out these large number cards that can be used for this activity and for many others.

Web Site

Math Playground

http://www.mathplayground.com

Online math games make learning engaging.

74 Graph Guides

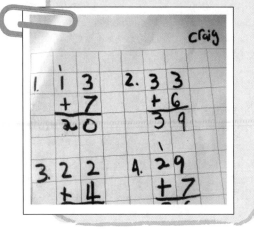

Materials

- Graph paper
- Pencil

Description

When considering adaptations for students with learning differences, start with the most basic. This idea of using graph paper as a visual support is one such basic idea that can make classwork much easier for the student to comprehend and the teacher to decipher.

There are likely many students in the classroom who will be able to work quicker and more effectively with graph paper, but learners who may benefit the most include those with fine motor planning difficulties, organizational problems, or low vision.

Graph paper can be chosen based on the age and needs of your students. Many sizes and background colors are available.

Directions

Introduce the use of graph paper to all students in your diverse classroom as a possible support for solving complex problems. By doing this, the students who most need to use it will not feel that they are being singled out and will understand that many learners may prefer using alternate materials.

This adaptation is most effective when students have to solve multistep problems and/ or line numbers up to add, subtract, multiply, or divide. It may also be useful for students working on geometry problems as the lined paper can serve as a cue for drawing straight lines.

Example

There were three students with learning disabilities in a ninth-grade algebra class. One student experienced dyscalculia and had a difficult time managing written work. She often struggled to keep numbers organized on the page in order to effectively set up and solve problems. She therefore used graph paper for in-class work and homework, which allowed her to follow lines horizontally or vertically to better organize her work. The two other students with learning disabilities sometimes used the graph paper, as did some of the students without disabilities. The graph paper was kept with other classroom supplies and was available at all times.

Reference

Brown, E. (2008). *Learning disabilities: Understanding the problem and managing the challenges.* Minneapolis, MN: Langdon Street Press.

Vendor

Incompetech
http://incompetech.com/graphpaper
Let students explore the many types of grid and graph paper available here.

Web Sites

National Center for Learning Disabilities
http://www.ncld.org
Information about dyscalculia and other learning disabilities is available through this web site.

Print Free Graph Paper
http://www.printfreegraphpaper.com
Free online printable graph paper is easily accessible.

75 Sticky Sticks

Materials

- Craft sticks
- Disc-shaped hook and loop tape

Description

So many manipulatives can be created right inside the classroom using materials available in your storage closet. If you already have craft sticks, these will take no more than a few minutes to assemble. They can then be used across lessons to teach about angles, line segments, nonstandard units of measurement, and even slope and intercept.

Directions

Put a hook and loop tape disc on each end of a stick. Push down to secure the discs.

Examples

Sticks were used in many geometry lessons by one 10th-grade math teacher. Students held up examples of obtuse, acute, and right angles; created polygons with their sticks; and even used them as visual supports for learning terms such as sine, cosine, and tangent.

Kindergarten students used sticks to "draw" and create story problems at a learning center. This was a novel and interesting way to learn for many students, but was particularly helpful for students with disabilities or fine motor problems who needed alternatives to writing, copying and drawing.

Keep in Mind

Many common materials can be used to create angles and shapes, including straws, stir sticks, pipe cleaners, spaghetti noodles, and licorice.

Reference

Simmons, K., & Guinn, C. (2001). *Math, manipulatives, & magic wands: Manipulatives, literature ideas, and hands-on math activities for the K-5 classroom.* Gainesville, Fl: Maupin House.

Vendor

Alison's Montessori

http://www.alisonsmontessori.com/Geometric_Stick_Material_p/m177.htm

You can purchase a geometry stick set here.

Web Site

Hands on Math in High School

http://handsonmathinhighschool.blogspot.com

Looking for more ideas for getting math out of the textbook and into the hands of students? If so, you will love this blog written by an innovative math educator. Search for lesson ideas, visuals, and DIY manipulatives.

76 Cardboard Dominoes

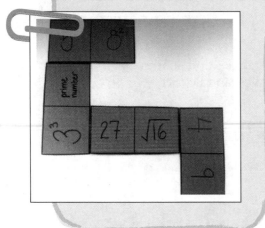

Materials

- Old boxes or sheets of cardboard
- Markers

Description

Dominoes are a great way to teach number values.

When we are looking for new ways to make the classroom less predictable and more playful, we often turn to classic table and board games for inspiration. Dominoes is one such game that can be adapted for use in the math classroom. We love that it can be used for very young children; dominoes for early grades might feature pictures, dots, and/or numbers 1–10. Dominoes for older learners can include numbers, equations, and vocabulary words.

Directions

To make the dominoes, create a template you can use to make all of the tiles. Trace your template repeatedly on sheets of cardboard and then cut your dominoes. Write your numbers or symbols on your dominoes or glue shapes down.

To have students play the game, copy and share these directions:

- Mix up the dominoes and place them face down on the table.
- Have each player draw six dominoes. If a game has more than three players, each player should draw three dominoes. Do not let the other players see your dominoes.
- The remaining dominoes are left on the table (these are the "sleeping" dominoes).
- The first player puts one of their dominoes down.
- The second player tries to put a domino on the table that matches one side of what is already there. If a player cannot go, the player picks a domino from the pile and skips that turn.
- Continue this process until someone wins. The winner is the first person to get rid of all of their dominoes. If no player can go out, the person with the fewest number of dominoes is the winner.

If you have students with multiple disabilities or sensory needs, you can add texture to your game by affixing foam stickers or other materials to some or all of the dominoes.

Examples

Algebra students created and played with equation dominoes as an introduction to simple functions.

Fifth graders made cardboard dominoes for their cross-age tutor partners in second grade. The sets served both as a final activity for the students and as a farewell gift at the end of the school year.

References

Dacey, L., & Eston Salemi, R. (2007). *Math for all: Differentiating instruction.* Sausalito, CA: Math Solutions.

Diller, D. (2011). *Math work stations: Independent learning you can count on, K–2.* Portland, ME: Stenhouse.

Storeygard. J. (2009). *My kids can: Making math accessible to all learners, K–5.* Portsmouth, NH: Heinemann.

Vendors

Didax

http://www.didax.com/shop/productdetails.cfm/ItemNo/5-595.cfm

You can purchase equation dominoes on this web site.

Learning Advantage

http://catalog.learningadvantagecatalog.com/advanced_search_result.php?keywords=dominoes

Many different types of dominoes are available here, including those that can be used to teach time, coins, and fractions.

Web Sites

The Cornerstone

http://thecornerstoneforteachers.com/free-resources/math/math-games-center-ideas

Angela Watson provides math game ideas for small-group instruction on her well-organized web site.

Helping with Math

http://www.helpingwithmath.com/printables/others/6rp1Fraction-Dominoes0.htm

Printable fraction dominoes are available.

Mathwire.com

http://www.mathwire.com/numbersense/dominoes.html

Mathwire offers activities for using dominoes in lessons.

77 Recycled Keyboard

Materials

- Old keyboard, calculator, or adding machine
- Magnets
- Glue

Description

This teaching idea allows students to use old materials in new ways. By removing the keys from a machine that has been long forgotten, teachers can bring a bit of quirkiness into the classroom and provide students with opportunities to both create and solve problems without having to write or verbally communicate.

Directions

Pry the keys off with your fingers. Wash them off to remove dust and dirt.

Add magnets if you want students to be able to manipulate the tiles on a board or other magnetic surface. Apply glue to the key and affix the magnet. Let the glue dry overnight.

Give to students to use in creating and solving problems, practicing facts, and answering teacher questions.

Example

Second graders used their recycled keys in a math center. Each group of students solved the problems left by the previous group and "wrote" new double-digit addition and subtraction problems for the next group.

Reference

Berkey, S. (2009). *Teaching the moving child: OT insights that will transform your K–3 classroom.* Baltimore, MD: Paul H. Brookes Publishing Co.

Vendor

Banks School Supply

http://banksschoolsupplycatalog.com/Number_Tiles-p-10059914.html

You can purchase 150 small number tiles and five tiles each of five different math symbols (addition, subtraction, multiplication, division, and equals) from this web site.

Web Site

Let's Play Math

http://letsplaymath.net

Let's Play Math offers fun ideas for teaching math to students of all ages.

78

Wipe-Off Flashcards

Materials

- Flashcards
- Small photo album
- Dry erase marker

Description

This idea is quick to assemble and ecofriendly. A wipe-off flashcard book can gives students opportunities to practice facts, work independently, check their own work, and tote their schoolwork or homework around in a back pocket. The book can also serve as a quick practice tool for early finishers or students who need more challenge in a particular concept.

We have used these books a lot for repeating homework assignments. They are especially useful for students with disabilities.

Directions

Collect a wide variety of flashcards. If you want students to practice concepts that are more sophisticated than those available on typical flashcard sets, you may need to print your own.

Place a flashcard into each sleeve of a photo-sized album.

Show students that they can write directly on the plastic pages and wipe answers off with a cloth.

Teach students strategies for using the books, including sorting the flashcards into groups based on their study strategies or commonalities (e.g., all of the *multiply by 0* facts together, all of the double digits together). They also may study with a peer and time each flashcard session to track progress over time.

Reference

Dillon, S. (2004). *Addition and subtraction flashcard games.* New York City, NY: Scholastic.

Vendor

Dollar Tree
http://www.dollartree.com/Math-Flash-Cards/p37598/index.pro
Dollar Tree sells flashcards in bulk.

Web Site

Fact Monster
http://www.factmonster.com/math/flashcards.html
Virtual flashcards help students practice.

79 Checkerboard Review

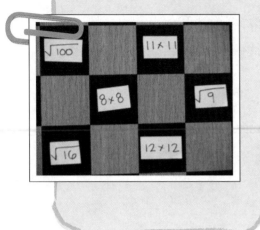

Materials

- Checkerboard
- Checkers
- Stickers
- Marker

Description

The game of checkers requires math skills all on its own, but you can add to the challenge by asking students to practice math facts or review terminology. Students play as they would in a typical game, but they have to think twice before moving to certain squares because they will be asked to answer a different question with every move they make.

This game is not only appropriate to play in the classroom, but it also can be shared with families on math night, parent–teacher conferences, or open houses.

Directions

Print math problems on small squares of paper and tape them down to either every square, half of the squares, or a few squares. Adding too many problems may slow down the game and annoy some students, so add the math problems based on the students' ages, abilities, and knowledge of checkers.

Example

Multiplication checkers was often a math activity choice for a young man on the autism spectrum. Instead of other assigned games or fact practice, he was regularly allowed to choose a partner and play during independent work time. Because playing board games such as checkers and chess was the student's favorite pastime, he was also allowed to play with the math facts board during indoor recess and Friday free time. Because he played so often, his teacher regularly switched the problems to make the game more challenging over time.

Reference

Lipp, A. (2011). *The play's the thing: Mathematical games for the classroom and beyond.* New York, NY: Anthem Press.

Vendor

Toys"R"Us

http://www.toysrus.com/family/index.jsp?categoryId=3252436

Shop here for checkerboards in different sizes and with different themes (e.g., storybook characters.)

Web Site

Math Games and Activities

http://www.mathgamesandactivities.com

Many ideas are offered for using games in the classroom.

80 Student-to-Student Tutorials

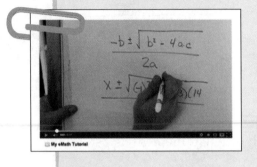

Materials

- Paper, interactive whiteboard, or dry erase board
- Computer
- Video camera
- Access to Internet

Description

Student-to-student videos harness the skills and talents of learners and put them in the role of instructor. Instead of the old-fashioned classroom presentation, this technique asks students to use the technology of their choice to create tutorials that will be available online to be viewed over and over again by classmates who need more support to master certain skills and competencies.

These tutorials are unique because viewers do not typically see the tutor in the clip; they merely see the work he or she is completing and hear the instruction. Therefore, students watching the tutorial get both a visual support and accompanying narration.

Directions

Show students several tutorials before having them make their own, so they can see common elements in the videos and figure out how to create the best possible product.

Assign students a concept to illustrate, an idea to teach, or a problem to solve. Remind them of any criteria, such as how long the clip should be and how many steps they need to illustrate.

Example

A high school math department asked every student to create a tutorial to share with classmates. Each video had to clearly illustrate the assigned concept and the narration had to include all necessary steps. Students were encouraged to use the tutorials as study supports and teachers used them to accompany lectures and discussions.

Reference

Khan, S. (2012). *The one world school house: Education reimagined.* New York, NY: Grand Central Publishing.

Vendor

Maplesoft

https://webstore.maplesoft.com

Software tools and programs to help students with classwork and homework.

Web Sites

AHS Academy

https://sites.google.com/a/austinisd.org/ahs-academy

Fantastic student-made videos that can be used in the classroom to support lessons and to teach learners about creating student-to-student tutorials.

Khan Academy

https://www.khanacademy.org

The library of videos at Khan Academy covers K–12 math, science, and humanities. Each video is approximately 10 minutes long.

Screenr

http://www.screenr.com

If you are a technology teacher and want students to teach and tutor about Internet use, software, or other related topics, check out Screenr. This site allows users to conduct and share free screencasts.

Study & Review

Contents

81	Customized Bingo Boards	196
82	Review Tower	198
83	Fortune Tellers	200
84	Hang-Ups	202
85	"Can You Guess?" Game	204
86	More-Than-Math Hopscotch	207
87	Memory Caps	210
88	Trading Cards	212
89	Stackables	215
90	Text Maps	217

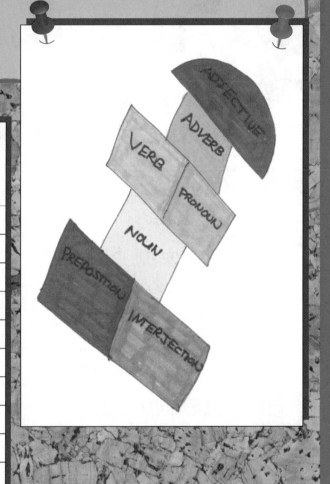

81 Customized Bingo Boards

Materials

- Heavy paper
- Images/clip art
- Printer
- Bingo markers

Description

Bingo is a game so familiar to most students of any age that rules don't even need to be taught. Therefore, it is easy to introduce to students of any age and takes little classroom time to set up. It is also a game filled with energy so it is the perfect antidote to a lackluster lesson.

Bingo can be used in many different ways in the classroom. A few games can introduce a bit of friendly competition while helping students become familiar with targeted content. Bingo can help students learn about a topic *before* it is taught. It is also a handy review tool.

Directions

Generate Bingo cards on the topic of choice. Because every student needs a different card, some teachers find it easier to present the pool of terms to students and make their own cards.

Cards can contain symbols, numbers, equations, pictures, diagrams, single words, letters, quotes, terms, or letters.

The teacher also needs a set of all of the possible choices or squares to use for a master set.

Decide on how students will need to play the game. You might have them simply identify what is called (e.g., *B*, Sandra Day O'Connor) and put a chip on it or you might have them solve a problem, translate a word, or otherwise answer a question in order to place their chip (e.g., *B*, the first woman on the Supreme Court).

As you call out each item, be sure to give students plenty of time to scan their cards. Many students will struggle to listen to the items and quickly check off their squares. For this reason, some teachers make each item available visually. So, each announced item might be posted on a card, dry erase board, projector, or interactive white board.

Let students know what they need to do in order to win the game. Are you using traditional rules where learners need to get a bingo down, across, or diagonally, or can they win with a "postage stamp" (four squares in upper right corner of card) or other shape? Also, do they just need to call out "bingo" and name their called squares, or do they need to provide evidence of their learning? In other words, do students need to define a word, reduce a fraction, or give an example of a metaphor?

When a winner is announced, the cards are cleared and play begins again.

Examples

Students in one American History class were often treated to a lively game of Bingo as an end-of-unit review. Students played Supreme Court Bingo, U.S. Senate Bingo, and Constitutional Amendment Bingo. A student with communication disabilities often served as the caller so he could work on a goal of "speaking clearly and comprehensibly" during a low-risk and meaningful activity.

An accounting teacher played bingo with his students several times a year. Students who called "bingo" had to not only call out the words or terms they had covered, but they had to correctly define and explain each one in order to win the game. Terms on the various student cards included *equity, interest,* and *liability*.

Reference

Cataldo, J. (2006). *Hands-on art activities for the elementary classroom.* San Francisco, CA: Jossey Bass.

Vendors

Bingo Card Creator

http://www.bingocardcreator.com

Printable bingo cards are available for a huge variety of subject areas, including 1930s America, geography, chemistry, types of whales, health food, and jazz artists.

Land of Nod

http://www.landofnod.com/multi-lingo-bingo/f895

Land of Nod offers Spanish and French bingo games.

Web Site

The Science Mom

http://the-science-mom.com/230/us-state-capitals-bingo-game

On this web site you will find a free download of a bingo game on U.S. state capitals.

82 Review Tower

Materials

- Stacking tower game
- Permanent marker and/or labels

Description

Students love to play familiar tabletop games in the classroom. This stacking tower game is always a winner because it involves a certain level of challenge for players of any age. It also has the potential to bring a bit of suspense and humor to a lesson.

Directions

Develop a series of questions, problems, or prompts relevant to your lesson or unit.

Using a permanent marker, write one question on each brick of each tower. You can also write each question on a label and affix it to the bricks.

Distribute the towers to small groups of students in your classroom and share these rules of the game:

- Students take turns easing bricks out the tower.
- As each learner selects a brick, he or she reads the question, problem, or prompt and provides an answer.
- If the student cannot answer, the player to his or her right can attempt to answer the question.
- Typically, in this game, the student who successfully grabs the last brick (before the tower topples) wins. In a modified version, you can have the student who collects the most bricks be the victor.
- Alternatively, you can have all students answer silently on paper for each question. At the end of the game, ask students to compare answers and total their scores.

Example

A high school Spanish teacher had students play this game to practice new vocabulary words. Every few weeks, students were asked to change the game themselves by identifying new words to study and affixing them to the classroom towers. Students were asked to include a set list of words and then add five new words of their choosing (either from old lists or from their own readings).

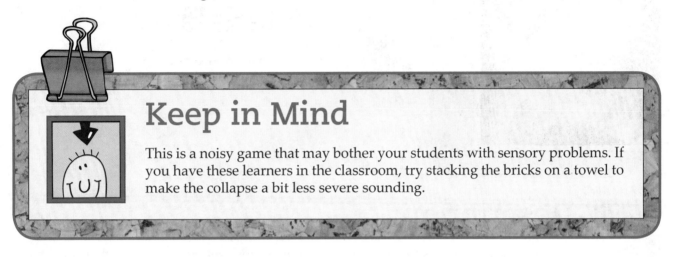

Keep in Mind

This is a noisy game that may bother your students with sensory problems. If you have these learners in the classroom, try stacking the bricks on a towel to make the collapse a bit less severe sounding.

References

Hoerr, T., Boggeman, S., & Wallach, C. (2010). *Celebrating every learner: Activities and strategies for creating a multiple intelligences classroom.* New York, NY: Jossey Bass.

Reyes, S., & Vallone, T. (2008). *Constructivist strategies for teaching English language learners.* Thousand Oaks, CA: Corwin.

Vendor

Hasbro

http://www.hasbro.com

On this web site from the creators of Jenga, you can read more about Jenga games and find out where to purchase them.

Web Site

The Board Game Family

http://www.theboardgamefamily.com

Although not a site specifically geared to teachers, The Board Game Family blog is a great source of game reviews and offers advice on games for different ages. They review card games as well as board games.

83 Fortune Tellers

Materials

- Tag board or heavy paper
- Markers

Description

Add a bit of playfulness to a review session by asking students to create their own paper fortune tellers. A fortune teller is a game piece created when students fold a piece of paper into an oragami-like sculpture that perches on top of their fingers. The game was originally designed to reveal fortunes that were hidden beneath small flaps. In the classroom, a fortune teller can be adapted for studying and review of key concepts.

The interactive nature of fortune tellers provides opportunities for collaboration and communication. Students needing support in these areas can practice skills like asking questions, providing one- to two-word answers, and turn taking.

Directions

To create your fortune teller,

- Fold a square paper into fourths.
- Then unfold the paper
- Fold over the four corners, evenly into the middle
- Fold into fourths again
- Flip the paper over
- Fold over the corners on the new side of the paper
- Fold into fourths one last time
- Once your fortune teller has been created, you are ready to play the game.

The student holding the paper is the fortune teller and he or she begins the game by asking the fortune seeker for a response of some kind. When the number is shared, the fortune teller opens and closes the paper while counting up to the selected number. When the counting stops, the fortune seeker is typically asked to select an inside flap. Typically a word or picture is featured on each flap. When a flap is selected, the fortune teller typically starts opening and closing the fortune teller again, this time spelling the chosen word (e.g., a-d-v-e-r-b).

Finally the fortune seeker is asked to choose one last flap, but this time the flap is opened to reveal a question. The student must answer the question correctly. If he or she cannot answer that question, the fortune teller shares the answer and it is his or her turn to now be the fortune seeker. To build in accountability, have students collect answers, questions, new words, or facts they receive as they work with partners. Then, have the students submit these learnings as an informal assessment.

Example

In a middle school science classroom, students had to design eight potential test questions for an upcoming examination on different systems of the body. The students illustrated and colored each segment of their fortune tellers. Then, they worked with partners for a few minutes at a time to ask and answer questions before moving on to new partners.

References

Schlemmer, P., & Schlemmer, D. (2011). *Teaching kids to be confident, effective communicators: Differentiated projects to get all students writing, speaking, and presenting.* Minneapolis, MN: Free Spirit.

Van Sicklen, M. (2009). *Origami on the go: 40 paper folding projects for kids who love to travel.* New York, NY: Workman.

Vendor

Dover Publications

http://store.doverpublications.com/0486478262.html

This origami kit has 15 premade fortune tellers with themes such as vacation destinations, outer space, music, and "gross stuff." Some of the fortune tellers are blank so they can be customized by the user.

Web Sites

Crafty Staci

http://craftystaci.com/2010/06/10/fabric-fortune-teller

This is a great tutorial on how to make a reusable cloth fortune teller.

Origami Fun!

http://www.origami-fun.com

This free paper-folding resource offers step-by-step instructions on how to create a complex design of your choice.

Origami USA

http://origamiusa.org

Devoted to the art of paper folding, this site features resources for purchase, design ideas, and forums for connecting with other origami enthusiasts.

84 Hang-Ups

Materials

- Wooden or cardboard door hanger
- Cardboard or tagboard
- Scissors
- Dry erase markers
- Laminating sheets/laminator

Description

Do you have students who respond to visual information better than they respond to auditory information? If so, you may want to incorporate hang-ups into your daily routine. Hang-ups can contain facts, questions, or simple reminders. For students that need to see to learn, hang-ups can provide a constant reminder of what is important. They also can provide a memorable way to learn content that is not part of the curriculum, such as book recommendations, study tips, jokes, or trivia related to class content.

Directions

Purchase a wood door hanger or make one by tracing an existing door hanger onto a piece of tag board or manila folder. Cut out your door hanger and laminate it.

Using dry erase markers, record the message and hang on the door.

You can also write your messages and then laminate your hang-up if you want to use it repeatedly. For example, hang-ups featuring vocabulary words, fun facts, challenge problems, or book and web site recommendations may be used year after year and even multiple times in one year.

Hang-ups are also a subtle way to respond to the diverse learners in your classroom. Use them to incorporate "getting to know you" facts about students (e.g., *Did you know that Sierra speaks Japanese?*), share trivia about student special interests (e.g., a Tour de France question for a student who loves to cycle), or offer special challenges to students needing enrichment (e.g., calculus problems hanging on the door of the algebra classroom).

Examples

An earth science teacher hung weekly questions on his door (e.g., *How has the earth changed over time?*) and used them to guide short classroom discussions each Friday. Often, students talked about the questions with classmates before the discussion even began.

A second-grade teacher used a different hang-up each day to remind students of social skills she was teaching in the classroom. She rotated signs that read *Sit with someone new at lunch today, Smile at your classmates today,* and *Give someone a compliment.*

An English teacher used a hang-up to highlight a new vocabulary word each week. He challenged students to slip the word into classroom questions or comments.

References

Balli, S. (2009). *Making a difference in the classroom: Strategies that connect with students.* New York, NY: Rowman & Littlefield Education.

Kluth, P. (2010). *"You're going to love this kid!": Teaching students with autism in the inclusive classroom.* Baltimore, MD: Paul H. Brookes Publishing Co.

Vendors

Amazon

http://www.amazon.com

You can search for *dry-erase door hangers* to find a handful of choices at different price points.

Craft Supplies For Less

http://www.craftsuppliesforless.com/kidscraftsupplies_doorhangers.html

An assortment of foam door hangers are on this web site.

Creative Teaching Press

http://www.creativeteaching.com/p-3977-where-are-we-door-hangers-mini-bulletin-board-set.aspx?catalog=120180

You can customize this set of door hangers.

Web Site

Izzy Share

http://www.izzyshare.com

If you are looking for more ideas on creating a responsive classroom and a welcoming space, search this site for different classroom spaces, designs, and displays by grade levels and themes.

85 "Can You Guess?" Game

Materials

- Hasbro's Guess Who? game boards
- Flashcards to cut up or cards to create your own images/words

Description

Many students have played Hasbro's Guess Who? In this popular table-top game, each player starts with a propped up board that is kept hidden from the player's opponent. The board contains 24 frames and inside each of these frames is a character with a unique name and physical characteristics. So "Howard" might have an orange bow tie and grey hair and "Leslie" might be a woman with curly hair and gold earrings. Each player has the same characters on their board.

The game starts with each player picking a card from a separate pile of cards containing the exact same 24 images. The object of the game is to be the first to figure out the character on the opponent's card by asking various yes/no questions. So, players take turns asking questions like, "Does this person wear a hat?" If the response to that question is a "yes," then all frames containing characters with hats remain upright. Those characters not wearing hats have their frames flipped down.

Players eliminate characters in this manner until all are left except one. At this point, a guess can be made and the game can be won.

In our version of the game, other content is substituted for the characters, but the rules essentially stay the same so that skills such as listening, asking questions, turn taking, reasoning, adding details, and communicating clearly can still be addressed.

Directions

Choose the content you want to teach. If students will have opportunities to use the game during free time, as homework, or repeatedly during daily lessons, be sure to target concepts and information that have high value. For example, you might choose colored shapes, figures in early American history, or simple machines.

Make three sets of cards: one set for each game board and one set for the draw pile.

As in the original version of the game, each player chooses a card from the draw pile and players take turns answering yes or no questions. Depending on what you are trying to teach, you may add additional rules. For instance, if you are playing the U.S. Presidents version, you might institute a rule that states *no guesses on looks or appearance,* so you can force learners to ask and learn about political affiliations, eras, assassinations, and so on.

Play continues until one of the players has narrowed their board to just one option. At this point, he or she makes a guess (e.g., "Is it Abe Lincoln?"). If the guess is correct, the game is over and the guesser wins. If the guess is somehow wrong, the other student wins. In this scenario, ask students to work together to assess where the error was made.

Examples

A fifth-grade teacher had students play the "Can You Guess?" game with animal classifications. Students could ask questions such as, *Does it fly?, Is it a mammal?, Is it a reptile?, Is it smaller than I am?,* and *Does it eat bugs?*

A science teacher created a game of "Can You Guess?" focused on the solar system. Students worked in teams of two to both generate and research potential questions before playing the games with their parents and siblings on family science night.

Students in a social studies class played the game using U.S. Presidents. The class first had to study both questions they might ask and the answers to those questions. The students used cheat sheets to ask and answer some questions, such as *Was he a member of the Whig party?* and *Did he serve two terms or more?*

Kindergarten students played a "Can You Guess?" game featuring pictures of all of the students in their classroom. All students loved to play the game and delighted in creating their own questions such as, "Does this person play blocks a lot?" The game was especially helpful for a student with Down syndrome who needed help learning classmate names.

References

Hinebaugh, J. (2009). *A board game education.* Lanham, MD: Rowman & Littlefield Education.

McLachlan, A. (2008). *French in the primary classroom: Ideas and resources for the non-linguist teacher.* New York, NY: Continuum International Publishing Group.

Vendors

Boardgames.com

http://www.boardgames.com

Games, games, and more games are available.

Junior Learning

http://juniorlearning.com/what-s-my-number-r.html

This game is similar to Guess Who?, except that it is completely math based. Students guess their opponent's number by asking questions, but the game can also be used to teach number patterns, operations, counting, and finding missing numbers.

Web Site

Hasbro Games

http://www.hasbro.com/games/en_US/guess-who

Hasbro not only makes the original Guess Who? game but has extended the product to include an electronic Guess Who? Extra edition, which includes a timer and yes/no button to answer questions. Hasbro also has many materials on their page, where you can download many free templates to adapt Guess Who?, including those featuring GI Joe, holiday themes, and dinosaurs.

86 More-Than-Math Hopscotch

Materials

- Sidewalk chalk
- Stones or other markers

Description

Do not leave hopscotch to only the littlest learners! Combine a refreshing trip outside with a review of facts, words, or concepts. Students can be practicing skills of balance, jumping, and hopping while studying standards-based content.

This lesson idea also gives students a little brain break because it incorporates movement and a change in classroom environment.

Directions

Create a game board or have students create their own.

Give each student a marker. You might have the marker be something related to your lesson. For example, if it is a science lesson, you could have the marker be a certain type of rock. If it is a math lesson, students might use dice or some type of manipulative.

The directions for the game are simple. However, many students may not know the actual rules for hopscotch, so even your older students may need a printed copy of these steps:

- Stand at the beginning of the board and toss your marker in the first square. Hop over square 1 (you must skip any spot that has a marker in it) to square 2.
- Hop through the grid on one foot unless there are two squares side-by-side, then you jump landing with one foot in each square.
- Hop to the end. Jump and turn around 180 degrees without leaving the grid. Hop back.
- Pause in square 2 to pick up the marker before finishing the board.
- Toss the marker in square 2, hop through the same way, then toss the marker in square 3, and so on.

You are considered "out" in any of the following cases:

- Your marker fails to land in the right square.
- You hop on a space that has a marker in it.
- You step on a line.
- You lose your balance when bending over to pick up the marker and put a second hand or foot down or hop outside the grid.
- You hop into a single space with both feet.

You then place your marker in the square where you will resume playing and the next player begins.

You might give students one chance to stay "in" by answering a challenge question from a deck of cards. This might be offered to each player once or twice per game.

The person who finishes the hopscotch board first wins.

In our version of the game, students also have to solve the problem, answer the question, or define the word in the segment where the object has landed.

Students or teachers can add new problems or words during the game if some teams seem to need additional support or challenge.

Examples

Third-grade students played multiplication hopscotch. As they jumped on each segment (e.g., 8 × 9), they had to shout out the problem's answer. If they didn't know the answer, they were "out" and had to start over. The most complicated problems (e.g., 12 × 12) were in the first squares so that all students could solve and hear others solve the same difficult problems repeatedly.

A classroom of sixth graders created elaborate hopscotches to practice vocabulary. They chose their own words from a list of 100 options. Half of the students functioned as designers and created hopscotch boards; the other half served as board "reviewers" and took turns trying out all of the different games.

References

Brewer, Z.J. (2010). *Math art: Hands-on math activities for grades 2, 3, and 4.* Charleston, SC: CreateSpace.

Hirsh-Pasek, K., Michnick Golinkoff, R., Berk, L.E., & Singer, D. (2009). *A mandate for playful learning in preschool: Presenting the evidence.* New York, NY: Oxford.

Singh, A. Uijtdewilligen, L., Twisk, J.W., van Mechelen, W., & Chinapaw, M.J. (2012). Physical activity and performance at school: A systematic review of the literature including a methodological quality assessment. *Archives of Pediatrics and Adolescent Medicine, 166*(1), 49–55.

Vendors

Crayola Store

http://www.crayolastore.com/category/draw-color/chalk

Crayola chalk, as well as tools to enhance your outdoor drawings, are accessible.

Hearthsong

http://www.hearthsong.com/product.asp?r=product_listing_ads&pcode=9021

If it is too cold to go outside, adapt this indoor hopscotch rug for your classroom.

Web Site

Peaceful Playgrounds

http://www.peacefulplaygrounds.com

Explore templates for a series of popular playground games.

87 Memory Caps

Materials

- Bottle caps
- Magazine pictures, drawings, or photographs
- Scissors or hole punch (check the size of your bottle caps)
- Glue

Description

Matching games—in which the objective is for players to take turns finding as many pairs as possible—are designed to teach associations and help students strengthen their memories. They are also inexpensive study tools to construct for or with students in K–12 classrooms. Students can play against an opponent or alone by timing each game and trying to beat their previous times.

Most memory games use cards. This version of the game, however, uses bottle caps, which can make pieces easier to grip for students with fine motor difficulties.

Directions

To create your game, collect an even number of the same-size bottle caps.

Scour your curricular materials to find words and images related to your content. When children are in lower grades, teachers often have them match two identical items (e.g., colors, sight words), but older learners should be given matches that require them to solve a problem or make an association. Students might have to match a Chinese word and an English word, an explorer's name and his or her picture, or two equivalent fractions.

Cut out and paste content into the inside of your caps.

To play the game, set the caps out in an organized array. Have students take turns turning over two caps at a time in search of a match. If they find two matching caps, they capture them and take another turn. If they overturn two unrelated caps, their turn is over. The player with the most caps at the end of the game wins.

Examples

Students in a Russian history class made memory games to study figures, places, and events. Every student-created game was slightly different, so students were encouraged to play with new partners each time. The students were given a few minutes to study before playing.

A fourth-grade peer tutor made a memory game for his first-grade tutee. Knowing that the young man was tiring of their usual flashcard routine, the tutor created a game that required players to match a single sight word with an image.

References

Diller, D. (2011). *Math work stations: Independent learning you can count on, K–2*. Portland, ME: Stenhouse.

Moscovich, I., & Stewart, I. (2006). *The big book of brain games: 1000 playthinks of art, mathematics & science*. New York, NY: Workman.

Vendors

Amazon

http://www.amazon.com

Amazon carries several different memory games including electronic versions.

Troll and Toad

http://www.trollandtoad.com/p306354.html

Troll and Toad has a memory game from USAopoly with a national parks theme.

Web Sites

Brain Matrix

http://www.brainmetrix.com/memory-game

Brain Matrix provides a free electronic memory game.

Discovery Communications

http://science.discovery.com/games-and-interactives/solar-system-memory-game.htm

On this site, students can play an interactive solar system memory game.

Flash Rolls

http://www.flashrolls.com/puzzle-games/science-lab-memory-match.htm

This virtual memory game features science equipment such as beakers, test tubes, and microscopes.

Spelling City

http://www.spellingcity.com/Games/line-match-with-definitions.html

This vocabulary matching game can be played online or printed.

88 Trading Cards

Materials

- Markers
- Heavy paper
- Keychain rings

Description

Trading cards can be created for real or fictional people, places, objects, events, or abstract concepts. They are a unique way to encourage studying both inside and outside the classroom and can be used across activities (e.g., classroom games, study sessions).

The using and exchanging of cards can be fun as well as educational. After all, most students will have seen (or even traded) baseball, basketball, or football cards, but few have likely had the chance to ask, "Got any Sir Isaac Newtons?" or "Trade you for your Sacajawea."

Directions

Choose an area of the curriculum with many related people, places, or ideas to study. For instance, sets of cards could be made for epic poets, the Underground Railroad, rainforest animals, epidemics, the Vietnam era, characters from *The Great Gatsby*, philosophers, geometric figures, or inventors.

Decide on content for both the front and the back of your cards. The front might have only a photo and the back might include your "stats" such as descriptive information, facts, and related illustrations.

Create the cards yourself or give students a list of cards they must create. You might designate a few that all learners must make and then allow for a few "free choice" options so that students can do a bit of research on their own and personalize their sets.

It is important to have students create multiple copies of their cards so they can trade them and use them in classroom activities.

Use the cards throughout the unit or even throughout the year. There are many different possible activities. For instance, you can have students trade cards, challenging each learner to collect the largest possible set. Then, play Monty Hall; on occasion ask, "Who has a _____ card in their desk/folder right now?" Give a gift such as a pencil topper, sticker, folder, or even a new trading card to that student.

Cards can also be used as handy study tools. Simply print, cut out the trading cards, and paste or tape the two sides together. Then laminate, punch holes in the top left corners, and place all of them on keychain rings. Invite students to flip through the cards when they have a few free minutes or give class time for quick peer quizzes every now and then.

Finally, you can reinforce content throughout the year by using your trading cards as a tool for grouping students. Simply have students select one of their cards and stand up holding the card. Then, ask the students to find two partners with different cards. When they get into their groups, have each learner share facts from their card before sitting down to work together.

Example

An art teacher had students create artist trading cards with facts about the artist on one side and an example of their artwork on the back. Students were encouraged to collect as many artists as possible by trading with those in their own class and with students in other classes as well. Students added to their decks by making their own artist trading cards, complete with their own artwork and biographies.

References

Fitzsimmons, J.M. (2012). Local species trading cards: An activity to encourage scientific creativity and ecological predictions from species' traits. *Journal of Natural History Education and Experience, 6*, 10–15.

Hong, X.S. (2005). *Trading cards to comic strips: Popular culture texts and literacy learning in grades K–8.* Newark, DE: International Reading Association.

Vendors

Doo Goods

http://www.doogoods.com/apps/webstore/products/show/3207825

This set of 30 trading cards includes a lesson plan manual and related printables. It is designed to help teachers build community in the classroom.

Lawrence Public Library

http://www.lawrence.lib.ks.us/2012/09/collect-all-seven

Librarians in Lawrence, Kansas, are selling banned books trading cards created by local artists. The cards are free to residents of Lawrence. Interested others can purchase them on the web site.

Web Sites

Classroom Freebies

http://www.classroomfreebies.com/2012/11/explorers-trading-cards.html

Download a free template for explorer trading cards.

National Aeronautics and Space Administration

http://science-edu.larc.nasa.gov/EDDOCS/Trading.html

Trading cards and lesson plans on atmospheric sciences are available.

National Geographic

http://education.nationalgeographic.com/education/activity/sea-creature-trading-cards

National Geographic allows you to print your own set of sea creature trading cards. Lesson plans are also available.

International Reading Association

http://www.readwritethink.org/classroom-resources/student-interactives/trading-card-creator-30056.html

This site is a must for any educator interested in using trading cards in the classroom. You can make your own sets using the tools on this site, as well as find ready-made lessons that cover almost every grade level.

89 Stackables

Materials

- Paper, plastic, or Styrofoam cups
- Stickers or pictures
- Markers
- Glue

Description

Stackables are manipulatives that can be used to teach relationships between ideas, concepts, or things. They are designed to teach a sequence, cycle, or hierarchy and can be used in social studies, science, math, and many other subject areas.

Directions

Create your stackables using any product you have available (e.g., Styrofoam, plastic, paper). Simply paste an image and word or phrase on each cup in the series. You may want to use a glue or sealant over the image to make sure that the graphics do not peel or move as students are stacking them.

If possible, create several different cup sets for the classroom so that students can review with different content. For example, you might use several different nesting cup sets created for food chains, with some having a hawk at the top of the food chain and some having a whale. You could also create some variety in geography stackables by using a variety of countries or by featuring different continents. Other ideas include place value, measurement (mile/yard/foot/inch), parts of a cell, and levels of government.

Example

During a study of ecology, a third-grade teacher created several different sets of stackables to teach her students about food chains. Students had to practice using the stackables provided and then create their own versions. The food chain stackables were particularly helpful in assessing the knowledge of a student with learning disabilities who struggled to demonstrate learning on quizzes and tests.

Reference

Kohl, M. (2010). *Art with anything: 52 weeks of fun using everyday stuff.* Lewisville, NC: Gryphon House.

Vendor

Party City

www.partycity.com

Plastic cups of every size and color can be found on this web site.

Web Sites

Differentiation Daily

www.differentiationdaily.com

Paula's blog is filled with easy-to-make learning materials. A new idea is shared every day.

Living Montessori Now

http://livingmontessorinow.com/2012/09/17/montessori-monday-diy-cosmic-nesting-boxes-map-towers-and-me-on-the-map

Deb Chitwood's site has many fresh teacher-tested ideas including these stackable geography towers.

90

Text Maps

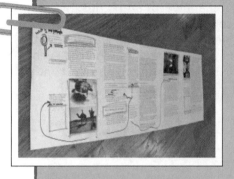

Materials

- Photocopies
- Tape or glue sticks
- Colored pencils, markers, or crayons
- Highlighters

Description

Text mapping-a technique popularized by educator Dave Middlebrook-will be new to many students and, therefore, interesting. Text maps are essentially book chapters reconstructed in scroll format to allow students to interact with content in a visually-interesting way. Scrolls are the last thing most students expect to see in their tech-rich classrooms, which, in part, is the attraction. Laying out the text in one large strip provides the opportunity for learners to literally see "the big picture" as they are introduced to new words, concepts and visuals. For those with comprehension struggles, this feature can be very helpful.

This strategy will be appreciated by students who like to interact with the text as they read beyond the occasional sticky note. With text mapping, students can use color, words, images, and symbols to identify important information and make connections between ideas.

Educators may find this technique helpful for teaching annotation, engaging in close readings, and encouraging collaborative study and review.

Directions

Make a copy of your textbook section or chapter, article, or story. Tape or glue the pages to each other to make a horizontal scroll, being sure to assemble the pages in a left-to-right direction. Place the maps on the floor for students to begin their work.

As students sit down to work, provide them with specific directions for the task. Keep in mind that the directions and focus might change with every map they create. Students might be instructed to find main ideas of paragraphs, preview the chapter and generate questions for study, review content previously studied, study the features of text, or identify critical words and phrases.

This technique can be differentiated for the diverse learners in your classroom. You might have students work in pairs and assign them roles. One student can be responsible for finding and highlighting main ideas, whereas the other can compare the content in the text with information found on the Internet or in trade books.

Example

A sixth-grade teacher had her students map out a textbook chapter on the Ming Dynasty, a subject completely unfamiliar to her students. She gave one copy of the chapter to each group of three learners and asked them to identify potential vocabulary words and terms, five main ideas, and three questions to ask other groups. They used colored markers and sticky notes to mark up the pages and added notes in the margins. One member of the team was designated as the "outside researcher" and was allowed to look up additional information on the events, people, and places featured in the text (e.g., Zheng He, the Forbidden City). This new content was added to the maps as well.

References

Greene, L.J. (2004). *Study max: Improving study skills in grades 9–12.* Thousand Oaks, CA: Corwin.

Porter-O'Donnell, C. (May, 2004). Beyond the yellow highlighter: Teaching annotation skills to improve reading comprehension. *English Journal*, 95: 82–89.

Rohde, M. (2012). *The sketchnote handbook: The illustrated guide to visual note taking.* San Francisco, CA: Peachpit Press.

Vendor

IKEA

http://www.ikea.com/us/en/catalog/products/20152281

This inexpensive scroll drawing paper is an ideal size for a mapping project.

Web Site

The Textmapping Project

http://www.textmapping.org

The Textmapping Project web site, which is completely dedicated to this method of instruction, is maintained by Dave Middlebrook, the educator who popularized this technique and currently conducts workshops on using it in the classroom. Middlebook is particularly interested in using text mapping to support students with learning disabilities who may need a more active and engaging approach to reading and notetaking.

Assessment

Contents

91   Desktop Displays 220

92   Censograms 223

93   Visual Rubric. 225

94   Comic Strip Check-In 227

95   Exit Slip Display 230

96   Tic-Tac-Toe Board 232

97   Notebooks 235

98   Kiddie Lit Creations 238

99   Multiple-Choice Fans 240

100 Teacher Report Cards. 242

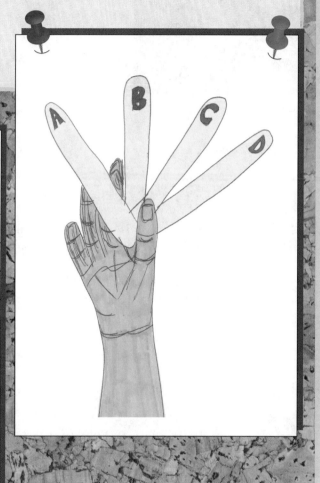

91 Desktop Displays

Materials

- Trifold presentation board
- Paper
- Markers
- Glue
- Letter/word stickers

Description

Desktop teaching is an active learning strategy designed to give students the opportunity to act as both teachers and learners. Students teach one another in a fair-like atmosphere; each prepares a lesson lasting from 5–10 minutes based on a topic or objective that is assigned to them or that they have chosen. Although this format works very well for formal presentations, such as those commonly associated with science fairs or final assessments, displays can also be used more informally to review or reinforce content after just a day or two.

Directions

Provide time for students to develop a short teaching sequence related to the subject at hand. Take some time to teach the students about good teaching. Encourage them to include visual aids and other learning materials, demonstrations, and short audience-participation activities in their lessons. In addition, it might be helpful to give them tips for staying within time limits, presenting information in a memorable way, and eliciting participation from their audience. You might even share some of the strategies in this book with your students. If possible, give students time to rehearse their lesson with a partner.

After students have their information prepared, have about half of the students set up materials on their desks for teaching, while the remaining students "visit" various lessons. Each learner typically chooses three or four lessons to attend in any one session. The "teachers" then conduct their lessons several times, beginning anew when each new audience arrives. The structure works best when a clear signal is given for the beginning and end of the lesson. This way, all of the rotations happen exactly at the same time and students can work on skills like time management and pacing. After several rounds of lessons, the other half of the class should be given an opportunity to set up their desktop lessons and the process begins again.

Example

Students in a seventh-grade industrial technology class used desktop displays as a way to showcase their learning at the end of the year. Each student in the class chose an independent study topic to explore in depth. As part of their desktop display, students were required to have at least one model or visual representation of their area of study and a short handout that their classmates could study and keep. Some of the desktop lessons developed were: tension and compression forces, bridge design, ancient technologies, and computer programming. Although beneficial for every active learner in the classroom, this hands-on structure was very helpful for the eight students in the classroom who were English language learners as these students were able to both hear and see the concepts being studied. Further, these learners were able to practice conversational English while engaged in academic work.

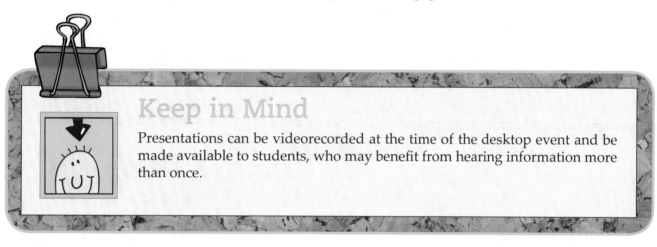

Keep in Mind

Presentations can be videorecorded at the time of the desktop event and be made available to students, who may benefit from hearing information more than once.

References

Draper, R. (1997). Active learning in mathematics: Desktop teaching. *Mathematics Teacher, 90,* 622–625.

Kluth, P. (2010). *"You're going to love this kid!": Teaching students with autism in the inclusive classroom* (2nd ed.). Baltimore, MD: Paul H. Brookes Publishing Co.

Vendor

Showboard
http://www.showboard.com
Showboard offers trifold project display boards in a variety of colors.

Web Site

Rethink Presentations

http://www.rethinkpresentations.com

This web site features many presentation tips and tricks to share with students. Although the intended audience of the site is adults who present professionally, much of the content is appropriate for sharing with students who are learning to present to peers and teachers. There are ideas for new technologies, using visuals, and dealing with nerves.

92 Censograms

Materials

- Chart paper
- Markers
- Circle-shaped stickers

Description

Censograms are visual representations of student ideas, preferences, opinions, or knowledge. They are designed for collaborative use. That is, everyone provides a response or responses which results in a snapshot of sorts of the group as a whole. Censograms are an especially helpful tool to use at the beginning of a lesson or unit to assess what learners know before designing upcoming activities.

Directions

Post questions or statements, or have students generate and post statements or questions. Give students (or small groups of students) round colored stickers to vote for their favorite answers. To visually track the responses, you might give each student, pair, or small group a different color to easily see how different learners answered.

Examples

During a unit on nutrition, a high school health teacher posted censograms around the room. Students had to provide an answer on each of the eight charts posted. Every censogram asked students to guess which of three meals or snacks was the healthiest. After they finished providing answers, the correct option was revealed.

Students in a fourth-grade class regularly used censograms to make predictions about the stories they read. Charts might ask students to guess whether or not certain events might occur or if characters would make certain decisions. The predictions were then reviewed after students finished reading the stories or passages.

Reference

Charlton, B. (2005). *Informal assessment strategies.* Portland, ME: Stenhouse.

Vendor

Bulk Office Supply

http://www.bulkofficesupply.com/colored-labels-laser-inkjet-color-coding.aspx
Round stickers in a variety of colors are available.

Web Site

Edutopia

www.edutopia.org
This blog, sponsored by the George Lucas Educational Foundation, is not focused only on active learning and formative assessment, but it is one of the best out there when it comes to information on those two topics.

93 Visual Rubric

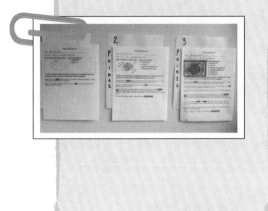

Materials

- Poster board
- Crayons or markers
- Tape or glue
- Work samples or photographs

Description

Rubrics have made it easier for many students to understand exactly what they need to do and know to achieve a particular score or grade. Some learners, however, may still be confused by the many descriptions featured on a rubric, especially if they are struggling readers, just learning English, or comprehend visual supports better than the written word. These students will appreciate the inclusion of visuals into a rubric and may even be able to provide a higher quality product because of this type of enhanced assessment tool.

Directions

Begin by designing your written rubric. Then, translate each step into a visual. This project may not be possible for every rubric you create, but it should work well for writing assignments, foldables or other graphic organizers, and study tools such as notebook entries.

Examples

Students in a middle school science class could check the visual rubric hanging in their classroom to see if their laboratory notes were complete enough to get the five points available. For instance, students could easily see that missing components, such as no diagram or image, would result in a missing point.

Second graders worked collaboratively to create their own visual rubrics. The teacher took them step-by-step through the creation of a short journal entry. The group wrote together and added the title, details, and punctuation together. They stopped at certain parts of the assignment to take a digital photograph of their work. Using this method, they could easily see all of the components they needed to add to each journal entry to get the highest mark available. Students were instructed to keep their rubrics in their notebooks so they had a daily guide for completing their journal work.

References

Arter, J., & McTighe, J. (2001). *Scoring rubrics in the classroom: Using performance criteria for assessing and improving student performance.* Thousand Oaks, CA: Corwin Press.

Stevens, D.D., & Levi, A.J. (2005). *Introduction to rubrics: An assessment tool to save grading time, convey effective feedback, and promote student learning.* Sterling, VA: Stylus.

Wilson, M. (2006). *Rethinking rubrics in writing assessment.* Portsmouth, NH: Heinemann.

Vendor

Teachers Pay Teachers

http://www.teacherspayteachers.com

The offerings on TPT change regularly; you will find hundreds of rubrics on the site for a range of grade levels and subject areas.

Web Sites

John A Dutton e-Education Institute

https://www.e-education.psu.edu/facdev/id/assessment/rubrics/rubric_builder.html

You will want to take some time experimenting with this electronic rubric creator offered by Pennsylvania State University.

Kathy Schrock's Guide to Everything

http://www.schrockguide.net/assessment-and-rubrics.html

Kathy Schrock's web site is one of the very best on rubrics.

94 Comic Strip Check-In

Materials

- Comic strip templates
- Colored pencils

Description

Comic book creations not only allow students to draw or create, but to learn a form of expression that may be new to them as budding artists. So many students are comic book fans, but it is unlikely that most have created their own strips or books. This activity, then, can be a rich opportunity to assess students while teaching them visual literacy skills such as how to read and write in pictures and how to pair visuals and text in a meaningful way.

Comic strip check-ins could be used for notetaking or assessing learners formally or informally.

Directions

Consider beginning your lesson by studying comics in general so that learners get a sense of the different types of art, the character types, and the various formats used. Then move to showing work samples of the types of comics you expect students to create.

You will want to be clear about the requirements as well as strategies for creating comics. Requirements may relate to neatness, length, type of content, and nature of dialogue. Strategies or techniques to be taught might include drawing characters, writing dialogue, storytelling, and storyboarding.

Examples

A middle school math teacher had a student who was seemingly unmotivated and failed to turn in assignments week after week. When the teacher told the student that she could hand in comic book creations as homework assignments (provided the concept taught in class was clearly explained in the drawings), she began turning in her assignments regularly and with enthusiasm.

Students in a ninth-grade English class were asked to do a retelling of Julius Caesar using unique characters (e.g., animals, monsters, fairies) and a comic book format.

A student with Asperger syndrome created his own social narratives using comic book boards and characters he designed. He wrote these stories to cope with new social situations, such as job interviews, school dances, and pep rallies.

References

Frey, N., & Fisher, D.B. (2008). *Teaching visual literacy: Using comic books, graphic novels, anime, cartoons, and more to develop comprehension and thinking skills.* Thousand Oaks, CA: Corwin Press.

Morrison T, Bryan G, Chilcoat G (2002), Using student-generated comic books in the classroom. *Journal of Adolescent & Adult Literacy, 45*(8), 758–767.

Moss, B., & Lapp, D. (2010). *Teaching new literacies in grades K–3: Resources for the 21st century classrooms.* New York, NY: Guilford Press.

Roche, A. (2011). *Comic strips: Create your own comic strips from start to finish.* New York, NY: Sterling Publishing.

Vendors

The Comic Book Project

http://comicbookproject.org

The Comic Book Project engages children in a creative process leading to literacy reinforcement, social awareness, and character development, then publishes and distributes their work for other children in the community to use as learning and motivational tools.

Dick Blick Art Materials

http://www.dickblick.com/products/canson-fanboy-comic-and-manga-papers

This virtual art store offers a variety of comic papers and comic boards.

Web Sites

Comic Book Daily

http://www.comicbookdaily.com

Comic Book Daily is dedicated to bringing a virtual comic shop environment to you. You will find discussions about comic books, a store, and several on-line comics.

Marvel

http://marvel.com/games/play/34/create_your_own_comic

Marvel has one of the best comic-book creating sites on the Internet. Students of all ages will love creating comics using familiar characters such as the Incredible Hulk and Captain America.

ReadWriteThink

http://www.readwritethink.org/classroom-resources/student-interactives/comic-creator-30021.html

Comic Creator is an interactive way for kindergartners through high school students to create their own comic strips online. Setting, characters, and dialogue are all elements that can be determined by the creator.

Stripgenerator

http://stripgenerator.com

Create your own comics and explore strips created by others.

95 Exit Slip Display

Materials

- Easel or large chart paper
- Designated bulletin board
- Index cards or sticky notes

Description

Exit slips are sticky notes or index cards that students submit at the end of a day or lesson to provide evidence of learning. They might answer a question, provide a reflection, solve a problem, or ask a question. Although this quick formative assessment tool may work well in some classrooms, other teachers see exit slips as a management problem. Teachers in middle and high school, in particular, may be left with hundreds of slips to sift through at day's end.

The exit slip display is an alternative to the collection of traditional exit slips. Instead of handing in a form or card to the teacher, students tuck or stick their response on a classroom board. Teachers can create a wall for the sticky notes or can handcraft a board (one for each class period if needed) with a small envelope or slot for each learner. This way, instead of having to collect and review all the slips in the pile of papers, the teacher only needs to skim the board to get a sense of what students understood or remembered, what misconceptions might persist, and what learning needs still exist. In addition, students can see the suggestions or ideas shared by classmates.

Directions

Many different types of exit slip displays are possible. A few ideas include the following:
- Dividing a poster board into sections with one area for each student
- Gluing library pockets to a poster board, with one numbered pocket designated for each learner
- Clearing a classroom wall for students to post sticky notes and group answers (when relevant)

Examples

Students in a middle school language arts class were asked to assign a trait to the main character of a novel and provide one piece of evidence from the text to support it. A child with limited vocabulary or expressive language delays was provided with a word bank of character traits to complete his slip.

Big questions are often used to check prior knowledge when introducing a new concept. In one social studies classroom, a teacher introduced a big question ("What is patriotism?") and then asked students to provide a one sentence response to post on a classroom exit display.

Keep in Mind

If certain students have difficulty writing or answering questions, the teacher can alter the assignment by providing that learner a sticky note that already contains a sentence starter or requires the learner to circle a response or fill in a blank with a single word.

References

Antonacci, P.A., & O'Callaghan, C.M. (2012). *Promoting literacy development: 50 research-based strategies for K–8 learners.* Thousand Oaks, CA: Sage.

Heacox, D. (2009). *Making differentiation a habit: How to ensure success in academically diverse classrooms.* Minneapolis, MN: Free Spirit Publishing.

Vendor

Really Good Stuff

http://www.reallygoodstuff.com/product/exit+pass+parking+poster.do

Don't want to make your own space for exit slips? Pick up this "exit slip parking lot" poster for a few dollars.

Web Site

ReadWriteThink

http://www.readwritethink.org/professional-development/strategy-guides/exit-slips-30760.html

Learn more about exit slips and how to use them in K–12 classrooms.

96 Tic-Tac-Toe Board

Materials

- Paper
- Pen/pencil

Description

Tic-Tac-Toe assessments are set up just like a typical game board, but feature an assignment or task in each square. To use this game in the classroom, teachers typically create a board and give students classroom time to choose and complete the activities.

Tic-Tac-Toe boards are ideal for the differentiated classroom because they give students the opportunity to study the same material as their classmates without having to necessarily engage in the exact same activities or have the same experiences. Every learner in your classroom, in fact, could study the material in a completely unique way while addressing the same unit goals or lesson objectives.

Different teachers may have different rules for using Tic-Tac-Toe boards, but many position the highest priority task in the center and require that learners complete any Tic-Tac-Toe path that includes that middle square. This still gives students choices, but provides everyone with at least one shared learning experience. This is different than the Tic-Tac-Toe game, so you will want to be sure to explain the rules clearly the first time you use your board.

Each item on a Tic-Tac-Toe board is typically completed and checked off by the teacher before the learner begins a new task.

Directions

To create your Tic-Tac-Toe board, first identify the outcomes and instructional focus of a unit of study. Then, use data, observations, conversations with learners, and student profiles to determine the needs, learning styles, and interests in your classroom.

Design nine different tasks. So that students will choose tasks based on their learning needs and interests instead of on length and ease, it helps to create nine tasks that are as similar in complexity as possible.

Arrange the tasks on the game board, keeping in mind that every student will have to use the center square. This task should be the most critical for all to experience.

Have students complete three tasks, one of which must be the task in the middle square.

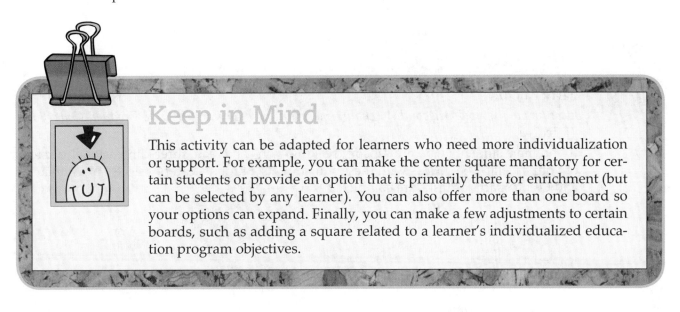

Keep in Mind

This activity can be adapted for learners who need more individualization or support. For example, you can make the center square mandatory for certain students or provide an option that is primarily there for enrichment (but can be selected by any learner). You can also offer more than one board so your options can expand. Finally, you can make a few adjustments to certain boards, such as adding a square related to a learner's individualized education program objectives.

Examples

A math teacher wanting to move beyond the textbook for his unit on statistics came up with a Tic-Tac-Toe board to kick off his unit. Students had classroom time to do research and engage in the related activities. Squares on his board invited students to watch a TED talk on statistics, explore a research article, and read a short page of statistics-related jokes and explain each in writing. These were completed before students started the unit as a way of getting them acquainted with the topic before studying it formally.

Eighth-grade science teachers used Tic-Tac-Toe boards to teach dominant and recessive traits. Some of the activities included conducting a classroom survey of three dominant traits; performing an Internet search to find two myths of human genetics, then using three reputable sites to confirm these myths; and contacting a person who has a career related to genetics or heredity and conducting a 15-minute interview on their work. The teachers worked with a handful of students to guide their choices, including two students with cognitive disabilities who had adapted forms with possible alternate choices for activities.

References

Westphal, L. (2009a). *Differentiating instruction with menus: Language arts (Grades 6–8).* Waco, TX: Prufrock Press.

Westphal, L. (2009b). *Differentiating instruction with menus: Math (Grades 6–8).* Waco, TX: Prufrock Press.

Westphal, L. (2009c). *Differentiating instruction with menus: Science (Grades 6–8)*. Waco, TX: Prufrock Press.

Wormeli, R. (2006). *Fair isn't always equal: Assessing and grading in the differentiated classroom*. Portland, ME: Stenhouse.

Vendor

Party Palooza

http://www.partypalooza.com/Merchant2/merchant.mvc?Screen=PROD&Product_Code=Foam TicTacToe

If you have students who are sensory seeking, you can create three-dimensional versions of your Tic-Tac-Toe boards with these squishy sets. Students can physically place their Xs and Os on spaces as tasks are completed.

Web Sites

Dare to Differentiate

http://daretodifferentiate.wikispaces.com/Choice+Boards
A variety of sample boards can be downloaded in different formats.

A Kid's Math

http://akidsmath.com/mathgames/ttmath/ttwhole.html
Try out this fun Tic-Tac-Toe game for students learning pre-algebra.

The Art of Education

http://www.theartofed.com/2012/07/11/how-to-use-choice-boards-to-differentiate-learning
We love this blog for art educators and were thrilled to see this individual post on using choice boards to differentiate. If you teach art be sure to grab this art history board and read all about the possibilities for using the Tic-Tac-Toe strategy in your classroom.

97 Notebooks

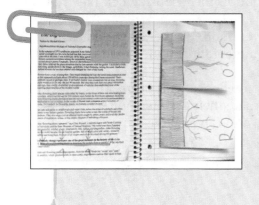

Materials

- Notebooks
- Pens, pencils, and highlighters
- Sticky notes

Description

In an era of high-tech learning, this throwback idea of educational journaling or scrapbooking is often welcomed by students who are artistic or enjoy hands-on experiences.

Notebooking can be used in any subject area and is typically used to help students and teachers track learning over time. Notebooks create a compilation of what has been learned, shared, or introduced in a certain subject or around a certain topic.

Students and teachers together typically decide what will be included in a unit or subject notebook, but products may include written notes, illustrations, lists, artifacts, maps, photos, charts, graphs, and communications such as letters and messages.

Notebooks typically contain both knowledge and personal reflections.

Possible entries across subject areas include:

- About me as a (learner/scientist/historian/reader)
- Questions I have about _____
- What I'm learning
- Lists of favorites (words/books/science-related movies/heroes in history)
- Stop and sketch
- Stop and jot (sticky notes)
- Stop and share (ideas from my partner)
- Student-created anchor charts
- Reflection on a lab/project/demonstration/presentation
- Graphic organizers of material
- Foldables
- Artifact and caption

Notebooking is a particularly wise choice in a differentiated classrooms because students can dive deeply into subject matter if they have the ability to do so. There are also many opportunities for students to personalize their learning by adding their own illustrations, finding artifacts to incorporate, and journaling about their work.

Directions

During a unit or throughout the year, work with students to construct their books. Entries can be made as a class or students can be directed to add to their books when they have ideas or artifacts to share.

Notebooks can be checked weekly, monthly, or even more frequently to ensure that learners are including necessary components and demonstrating understanding of the subject matter.

Give students regular opportunities to share their notebooks with peers. This type of sharing can help students clear up misconceptions, compare their understanding of a topic with someone else's understanding of that information, and can provide opportunities for teaching and learning.

Example

A ninth-grade biology teacher used notebooking during the entire year. Students used them nearly every day. The notebook was a space for documenting learning, interacting with content, and studying for quizzes and tests. Students used notebooks to solve problems, work with graphs and diagrams, design graphic organizers, write responses to laboratory work, and more.

References

Buczynski, S., & Fontichiaro, K. (2009). *Story starters and science notebooking: Developing children's thinking through literacy and inquiry.* Westport, CT: Teacher Ideas Press.

Daniels, H., & Bizar, M. (2005). *Teaching the best practice way, methods that matter, K–12.* Portland, ME: Stenhouse.

Klentschy, M.P. (2010). *Using science notebooks in middle school classrooms.* Arlington, VA: NSTA Press.

Marcarelli, K., & Bybee, R.W. (2010). *Teaching science with interactive notebooks.* Thousand Oaks, CA: Corwin.

Rivard, L., & Straw, S. (2000). The effect of talk and writing on learning science: An exploratory study. *Science Education, 84*(5), 566–593.

Shepardson, D., & Britsch, S. (2001). The role of children's journals in elementary school science activities. *Journal of Research in Science Teaching, 38*(1), 43–69.

Vendor

Notebooking Pages

http://notebookingpages.com

This homeschooling mother sells journal materials for different topics (e.g., animals, U.S. states) and provides many resources for introducing notebooking across subject areas.

Web Sites

Science Notebooks

http://www.sciencenotebooks.org

This web site, which is supported by the National Science Foundation, is designed to help teachers set up a science journaling classroom.

Science Notebooking

http://sciencenotebooking.blogspot.com

This fantastic blog provides many ideas for successfully using science notebooking in the classroom. Blogger Eve Heaton is also a technology expert, so expect to find plenty of tips for using interactive whiteboards, e-tablets, web sites, and digital cameras in your lessons.

The Middle School Mouth

http://themiddleschoolmouth.blogspot.com/2012/05/more-on-my-social-studies-interactive.html

Follow this seventh grade teacher's journey with interactive social studies notebooks. "Seldy" is a veteran educator who shares a lot of work samples on his site and invites teachers both take ideas and share them with one another.

98

Kiddie Lit Creations

Materials

- Blank books
- Markers
- Photographs, illustrations, and stickers

Description

The best way to learn something may be to teach it to someone else. If this is true, kiddie lit creations may be the key to comprehension for some of the learners in your class.

By having students create books for children using standards-based content, you can assess whether or not they can identify the most relevant points, break them down into meaningful chunks, and explain them in terms that someone without experience or background in the topic could understand. Therefore, kiddie lit creations can serve as both meaningful and unique assessment tools.

Directions

To begin, identify concepts that should be used in the literature project. Provide students with this information and give them basic guidelines for writing and illustrating. For example, you might require a certain number of pages, the inclusion of a handful of vocabulary words, and a clear presentation of a theme, idea, or problem.

Provide plenty of examples of children's literature so learners can get ideas for illustrations, storytelling techniques, organization, and book formats. Some students may want to design pop-up figures, others may take and use photographs, and still others may want to create paper collages, paintings, or drawings.

Students can work on kiddie lit creations on their own or with partners.

Examples

Biology students created ABC books on the topic of matter. Certain terms had to be highlighted (e.g., Bohr model), but students could also choose some terms not on the master list.

Students had opportunities before test day to share their books with peers and to use them in question-and-answer sessions with partners.

Ninth-grade students designed kiddie literature to teach about one aspect of the American Revolution. Students could choose to teach the Stamp Act, the Boston Massacre, the Boston Tea Party, Lexington and Concord, or the Battle of Bunker Hill. Students took turns sharing their creations in small groups and then reading them to local elementary school students via Skype. For one student in the class with multiple disabilities, this activity served as an opportunity to practice his emerging reading skills in a meaningful context.

Reference

Leedy, L. (2005). *Look at my book: How kids can write and illustrate terrific books.* New York, NY: Holiday House.

Vendor

Bare Books
http://www.barebooks.com
You can find dozens of different types of blank books including some with cover art that can be colored.

Web Sites

Jim Harris
http://www.jimharrisillustrator.com/ChildrensBooks/TipsforIllustrators.html
Jim Harris offers several tips for young illustrators.

The National Writing Project
http://www.nwp.org/cs/public/print/resource/922
These resources can help in teaching all aspects of writing.

99 | Multiple-Choice Fans

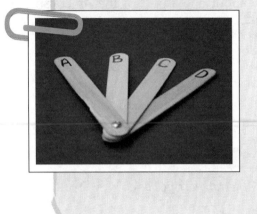

Materials

- Craft sticks
- Screws
- Washers
- Colored markers

Description

Do you want to engage in a speedy classroom assessment while also helping your students prepare for tests and quizzes? Create these spiffy little answer fans to keep discussions interactive and to conduct an ongoing assessment of what students know and understand. Instead of calling on one student at a time to assess learning and understanding, you can "hear" from all students at once by asking every learner in the classroom to hold up an answer to your multiple-choice question.

You can use your multiple-choice fans just one or two times to start a lesson, or you can integrate them into an entire lecture, discussion, or classroom activity.

Directions

Decide how many choices you want your students to have and assemble groups of craft sticks in that amount. Write the letters or numbers you will need on one end of the sticks, and drill or punch a hole in the other end of the sticks. Attach the sticks together with the screw and washer, leaving it loose enough so that the sticks can be moved easily.

Before you start teaching, decide on a handful of questions that can add interest to the lesson. Questions might be simple polls that provide information about student interests or viewpoints, such as "What is your favorite season?" You also can include factual questions, such as "Which U.S. president was impeached?" or "What is radial symmetry?"

The activity works best when the questions and potential answers are displayed visually on a dry erase or interactive whiteboard.

Example

A class of sixth graders prepared for all of their math tests by submitting sample multiple-choice questions for study. The questions were presented by the individual authors and the correct answers were given after a survey of the class was taken. The questions that had the most incorrect answers were repeated after a short explanation of the correct answer by the teacher.

References

Duncan, D. (2005). *Clickers in the classroom.* Boston, MA: Addison Wesley.

Penuel, W.R., Boscardin, C.K., Masyn, K., & Crawford, V.M. (2007). Teaching with student response systems in elementary and secondary education settings: A survey study. *Educational Technology Research and Development, 55*(4), 315–346.

Vendors

iClicker

http://www.iclicker.com

If you have the funds, go for the high-tech version of this tool and let students punch in their answers during daily lessons.

Poll Everywhere

http://www.polleverywhere.com/classroom-response-system

This classroom response system uses cell phones.

Web Sites

The Carl Wieman Science Education Initiative at the University of British Columbia

http://www.cwsei.ubc.ca/resources/clickers.htm

Hundreds of clicker questions that are appropriate for secondary education science classes.

The Carroll College Department of Mathematics, Engineering, and Computer Science

http://mathquest.carroll.edu

Visit this site to find a variety of math questions for college-level classes, which can be adapted for use in the secondary education classroom.

Engaging Technologies

http://www.engaging-technologies.com/clicker-activities.html

Activities and questions for all ages are on this web site.

100 Teacher Report Cards

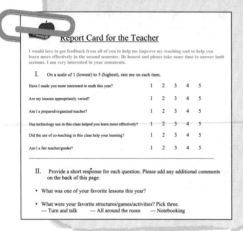

Report Card for the Teacher

I would love to get feedback from all of you to help me improve my teaching and to help you learn more effectively in the second semester. Be honest and please take some time to answer both sections. I am very interested in your comments.

I.   On a scale of 1 (lowest) to 5 (highest), rate me on each item.

Have I made you more interested in math this year?	1	2	3	4	5
Are my lessons appropriately varied?	1	2	3	4	5
Am I a prepared/organized teacher?	1	2	3	4	5
Has technology use in this class helped you learn more effectively?	1	2	3	4	5
Did the use of co-teaching in this class help your learning?	1	2	3	4	5
Am I a fair teacher/grader?	1	2	3	4	5

II.   Provide a short response for each question. Please add any additional comments on the back of this page.

• What was one of your favorite lessons this year?

• What were your favorite structures/games/activities? Pick three.
--- Turn and talk   --- All around the room   --- Notebooking

Materials

- Cards or paper

Description

At its core, differentiation is about knowing your students and what works for each of them. What better way to learn about the needs of your learners than to ask them to rate you and your teaching?

This assessment tool may feel risky to some educators, but it can also be very rewarding. You position yourself to learn about which types of lessons are working well, which assessments students see as useful, and which classroom games and activities students see as meaningful, enjoyable, and effective.

Add teacher report cards to your menu of assessments to get to know your learners even better and to see what teaching looks and feels like on the other side of the teacher's desk.

Directions

Decide on what kind of feedback would be most useful to you personally and to your teaching. Then, create items that will be easy for students to answer. You could use a Likert scale for some items (i.e., a scale of 1–5) or multiple-choice items. These tools will let you see if there are themes that emerge. For example, if all learners give you a 1 or 2 in *I get enough opportunities for movement*, you know that this area is in need of improvement.

You will also want to leave some space for evaluator comments because you can likely learn the most from open-ended feedback. You might ask questions such as, *What was your favorite lesson so far?*, *What is one thing you wish we could do more often?*, or *What games, activities, or review exercises are the most helpful?* You can ask students to keep their names off the reports to encourage honesty.

After collecting and reviewing the reports, consider sharing results with your students and letting them know about any comments or information that made you feel good or satisfied. You also can report on any changes you intend to make as a result of the feedback.

Example

In his algebra and geometry classes, a high school math teacher gave his students a mid-year teacher report card. He was rated on his sense of humor, the clarity of his teaching, and the amount and quality of homework.

Reference

Byrnes, M.A., & Baxter, J. (2012). *There is another way: Launch a Baldridge-based quality class-room* (2nd ed.). Milwaukee, WI: Quality Press.

Vendor

Grainger

http://www.grainger.com/Grainger/QUALITY-PARK-Report-Card-Jacket-23L193

Make it official with report card jackets that can be used month after month or quarter after quarter.

Web Site

Education World

http://www.educationworld.com/a_lesson/05/lp345-03.shtml

A lesson plan is provided for designing teacher report cards.

BROOKES
PUBLISHING Co
www.brookespublishing.com

Professional development DVD—see how real inclusive schools work!

"You're Going to Love This Kid!"
A Professional Development Package for Teaching Students with Autism in the Inclusive Classroom

By Paula Kluth, Ph.D.
A Film by Landlocked Films

US$129.95 | Stock Number: BA-72049
2012 • 9 x 12 folder w/ 32-page saddle-stitched booklet and 71-minute DVD

What if your school just said "yes" to inclusion? How would students with and without autism benefit? How would you solve the challenges? What do great inclusive schools really look like? Paula Kluth has the answers—and now they're on one powerful DVD that will help make your school an inclusion success story.

One of today's most dynamic, respected, and in-demand experts on autism and inclusion, Paula Kluth brings together more than a dozen of her colleagues for this complete professional development package on effective inclusion. Hosted by Paula and expanding on key lessons from her bestselling books and popular presentations, the **55-minute video** walks you through the what, why, and how of honoring and supporting all learners. Through clips of real teachers in successful inclusive classrooms and interviews with educators, administrators, a parent, and students, you'll discover practical ways to

- differentiate instruction
- nurture students' social skills through peer supports
- improve school culture so all students are welcomed and included
- individualize objectives and standards
- make the most of each student's gifts and interests
- use positive behavior supports
- presume competence
- strengthen partnerships between schools and families
- co-teach effectively
- reframe challenges in a positive way

❏ **55-minute video** with teaching strategies, classroom clips and interviews, and an inside look at 3 sample lessons

❏ **16-minute video,** *Speaking of Inclusion: Ten Questions Asked and Answered,* an inclusion Q&A with the education professionals in the feature film

❏ **Facilitator's Guide** with sample professional development plans, summaries of teaching strategies, questions for group discussion, and more

❏ **Practical forms and checklists** to evaluate practices and plan

An ideal professional development resource for experienced educators and preservice teachers in K–12 classrooms, this package also includes a concise **Facilitator's Guide** with sample professional development plans, helpful summaries of teaching strategies, more tips from educators, thought-provoking questions for group discussion, and **practical forms and checklists** to evaluate practices and plan supports.

Say yes to inclusion with this comprehensive guide from Paula Kluth—and help your school become a stronger community where all learners use their unique gifts and achieve their full potential.

See the next page for MORE bestsellers from Paula Kluth!

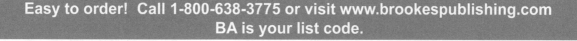

Easy to order! Call 1-800-638-3775 or visit www.brookespublishing.com
BA is your list code.

More bestsellers from Paula Kluth!

Help *all* students reach their full potential with these must-have practical books!

A Is for "All Aboard!"
By Paula Kluth, Ph.D., & Victoria Kluth

The first alphabet book created with children with autism in mind, *A Is for "All Aboard!"* fosters literacy using a common fascination—trains.

US$16.95 | Stock #: BA-70717 • 2009 • 32 pages • 11 x 8.5 • hardcover • ISBN 978-1-59857-071-7

"You're Going to Love This Kid!"
Teaching Students with Autism in the Inclusive Classroom, *Second Edition*
By Paula Kluth, Ph.D.

The second edition of the bestselling inclusion guide—now with photocopiable forms, checklists, and planning tools.

US$36.95 | Stock #: BA-70793 • 2010 • 368 pages • 8.5 x 11 • layflat paperback • ISBN 978-1-59857-079-3

From Tutor Scripts to Talking Sticks
100 Ways to Differentiate Instruction in K–12 Inclusive Classrooms
By Paula Kluth, Ph.D., & Sheila Danaher, M.S.Ed.

Differentiated instruction is fun and easy with this practical K–12 guide, packed with 100 teacher-designed, kid-tested adaptations.

US$39.95 | Stock #: BA-70809 • 2010 • 296 pages • 8.5 x 11 • paperback • ISBN 978-1-59857-080-9

"Just Give Him the Whale!"
20 Ways to Use Fascinations, Areas of Expertise, and Strengths to Support Students with Autism
By Paula Kluth, Ph.D., & Patrick Schwarz, Ph.D.

Give teachers a powerful new way to think about students' "obsessions": as positive teaching tools that calm, motivate, and improve learning.

US$19.95 | Stock #: BA-69605 • 2008 • 160 pages • 8.5 x 11 • paperback • ISBN 978-1-55766-960-5

Pedro's Whale
By Paula Kluth, Ph.D., & Patrick Schwarz, Ph.D. | Illustrated by Justin Canha

A simple, eye-opening story based on the real event that inspired *"Just Give Him the Whale!,"* this book is a great way to get everyone on board with inclusion.

US$18.95 | Stock #: BA-71608 • 2010 • 32 pages • 8 x 8 • hardcover • ISBN 978-1-59857-160-8

"A Land We Can Share"
Teaching Literacy to Students with Autism
By Paula Kluth, Ph.D., & Kelly Chandler-Olcott, Ed.D.

Go beyond functional literacy skills and bring meaningful literacy instruction to K–12 students with autism.

US$29.95 | Stock #: BA-68554 • 2008 • 248 pages • 7 x 10 • paperback • ISBN 978-1-55766-855-4

Follow Paula Kluth on Facebook • Bookmark Paula's websites: paulakluth.com and differentiationdaily.com

Easy to order! Call 1-800-638-3775 or visit www.brookespublishing.com
BA is your list code.